THE
PORTABLE
WRITER

A Brief Manual of Style, Usage, and Mechanics

Second Edition

Hilary Russell

Berkshire School

WAYSIDE PUBLISHING
Suite 5, 11 Jan Sebastian Dr
Sandwich MA

Cover by Ronn Cabaniol

Thank you to Scott Barker, Cornelia Baskin, Linda Bellizzi, Jane Bragdon, Ronn Cabaniol, Jo Chaffee, Elizabeth Clifford, Steve Craig, Heather Forrest, John Hornor, Bayard Kellam, Judy Magenis, John McKenna, Norman Merrill, Sue Montgomery, Sally Morgan, Procter Smith, Janice Thomas, John Toffey, and Charlotte Wilson. Thanks also to Richard Lederer for his aid and advice and for allowing me to use sentences from his book *Anguished English* (Wyrick & Co.).

I am also grateful to the following student writers for allowing me to use excerpts from their work as examples of good writing: Jen Airoldi, Lisa Arkfeld, David Hart, George Mack, David Nute, Mike Raleigh, Joe Roland, Josh Scala, and Lee Scharge.

Excerpt from "Digging" from *Poems 1965-1975* by Seamus Heaney, copyright © 1966, 1980 by Seamus Heaney. Reprinted by permission of Farrar, Strauss, and Giroux.

Excerpt from "The Love Song of J. Alfred Prufrock" in *Collected Poems 1909-1962* by T. S. Eliot, copyright © 1936 by Harcourt Brace Jovanovich, Inc., copyright © 1963, 1964 by T. S. Eliot, reprinted by permission of the publisher.

© Copyright 1998 by Wayside Publishing

PRINTED IN THE UNITED STATES OF AMERICA

ISBN 1-877653-47-0

CONTENTS

ABOUT THIS BOOK

The Portable Writer is a manual of style, a reference book for usage and mechanics, and a review book for standardized tests. As a manual of style, it helps students to do the following:

- begin papers by listing ideas and free writing
- understand the differences between personal writing (autobiographical and fictional topics) and academic writing
- establish a voice
- provide detail
- write clear, concise, varied sentences
- organize academic papers logically
- understand the power of tense and point of view in personal writing
- edit and revise

Since this book can be snapped into a three-ring notebook, English students can keep *The Portable Writer* on hand to improve papers in progress and to correct papers as soon as they are returned. Also, teachers who conduct writing classes as workshops will appreciate the fact that students can easily bring *The Portable Writer* to class daily, in case there is a question about usage, style, or mechanics.

The Portable Writer not only provides a review of grammar but also functions as a composition and usage text, offering explanations, writing exercises and practice sentences. Its central purposes are to illustrate the principles of good writing, to help students correct their errors intelligently and efficiently, and to aid the review for standardized examinations, such as the A.C.T. (The American College Testing Program), the College Board Achievement Test in English Composition, and the Test of Standard Written English section of the Scholastic Aptitude Test.

Hilary Russell

The Portable Writer

BEGINNING A PAPER

> *Get it down. Take chances. It may*
> *be bad, but it's the only way you*
> *can do anything good.*
> William Faulkner

When William Faulkner says, "Get it down. Take chances," he suggests that you, a writer beginning a paper, should not worry if you are unsure of exactly where your ideas are headed. Start writing about a point that interests you, push it as far as you can, and then question where to go next. Usually this process, called **free writing**, will uncover new points, clarify old ones, and lead your thoughts in a new direction. So as you begin, don't worry about having a well-developed outline; that can come later after you have done enough free writing to discover what you want to say. Instead, work from a list of a few rough ideas.

The more free writing you do, the better. It will increase your chances of discovering new ideas and will give you plenty of material to return to later.

TWO KINDS OF WRITING

Between my finger and my thumb
The squat pen rests.
I'll dig with it.

Seamus Heaney

Most English teachers assign two kinds of papers – personal and academic. The first is usually easier for students because the subject matter is theirs. In other words, when a teacher assigns a journal entry, an autobiographical sketch or a short story, you write about yourself – your ideas, your memories, your imaginings.

On the other hand, when your teacher asks you to write about the central theme in Nathaniel Hawthorne's *The Scarlet Letter* or to discuss Frederic Henry's love for Catherine in Ernest Hemingway's *A Farewell to Arms*, he or she forces you outside yourself. You cannot **write** until you have **read** and **understood**. In academic writing you have to master the material before you write; in personal writing your experience – real and imaginary – is the material.

THE CHARACTERISTICS OF PERSONAL WRITING

- ◆ You write the way you actually think. Consequently, your reader hears a comfortable tone of voice coming through your writing instead of your idea of how a good student sounds. ("This point clearly illustrates that Frederic Henry has become disillusioned ...")

- ◆ Because you write in a natural tone of voice or one

2

that you understand (maybe you are good at writing the way a child talks because you have younger brothers or sisters who never stop talking), you use vocabulary, sentence structures, and patterns of thought that feel comfortable. You begin to develop, therefore, **your own style**.

◆ Since you probably have a genuine interest in the subject of your paper, you ask yourself if your reader will understand what you mean, and if you will need to give him more physical detail to see, hear, taste, touch, and smell.

◆ When you discover that what is funny or sad or frightening to you is not so to your reader, you will try to understand why your passage doesn't work, and you will probably learn something about writing, and about yourself.

CHARACTERISTICS OF ACADEMIC WRITING

◆ Academic papers teach you to write according to a set of conventions that help make your ideas clear and your arguments persuasive. These conventions – like manners, tuxedos, and formal dresses – may inhibit you until you get used to them and become at ease within their limits. Then you will use them with style and confidence.

The Conventions of Academic Writing

◆ Use a direct, informative title. (Don't be cute or misleading.) Do not underline or quote your own title in any paper – academic or personal.

TITLE

3

◆ Avoid the first person singular – **I, me, my, mine**. Instead, say "the reader," "this reader," "one," or "we."

◆ Refer to living authors by their full names (Ann Tyler, John Updike) or by title (Ms. Tyler or Mr. Updike) and to deceased authors as above or by their last names (Whitman, Dickinson). Never call authors, living or deceased, by their first names.

◆ Refer to characters by the same names that their authors use. Say Catherine, not Kitty or Kate, because no character in *A Farewell to Arms* calls Catherine "Kitty" or "Kate."

◆ Write about literature in the present tense. After all, Macbeth **is** and he always will be in the present as long as people see or read Shakespeare's play. Say, therefore, "When we first **see** Macbeth . . . " and "Later he **orders** the death of Banquo."

◆ Use formal English. Specifically, avoid **sentence fragments**, **contractions**, **slang**, and **informal usages**. For example, "Freddie got all mixed up about all that shooting" is informal, while "The immorality of war disillusions Frederic Henry" is formal.

◆ Academic papers **prove something**: that you know the plot, that you understand the concepts, that you can analyze, synthesize, and summarize. You have to know the facts and be able to present them as **proof** of your **idea**. Later in this book, you will learn more about getting ideas and proving them.

◆ In an academic paper, you provide the reader with examples from the text for the same reason that you

4

describe images (sights, sounds, smells, etc.) in personal writing – to **show** the reader what you mean. For instance, which is more convincing, "Macbeth feels guilty" or "In his extreme guilt, Macbeth asks, 'Will all great Neptune's ocean wash this blood/Clean from my hands?' " The quotation convinces us for two reasons:

1. It says that Macbeth feels so guilty that he thinks all the oceans do not hold enough water to wash the blood from his hands.

2. It gives us something to **see** – blood, hands, water, oceans. Isn't it easier to remember a **thing** than a **feeling** such as guilt?

◆ Just as personal writing teaches you about yourself, academic writing teaches you about the text. Do you know the feeling of getting to the end of an academic paper and discovering that you have contradicted your original idea? We contradict ourselves in early drafts of papers because as we write, our thinking turns and ends up in unexpected places – usually on washed out roads and dead ends, but sometimes on beautiful short cuts to ideas we had never thought of before. Since we want to bring these ideas to the center of our papers, we have to rethink and revise.

WRITING IN GENERAL

As Seamus Heaney tells us, writing is digging with a pen (or a typewriter or a word processor) to uncover and clarify feelings, ideas and relationships. Since both personal and academic writing involve this digging with words, why keep these two kinds of writing apart? Why should there be a gap between the comfortable personal paper and the threatening academic paper? Why not, so to speak, dig in the middle ground? Here are some ways you can work that ground:

◆ Write an informative essay about a non-academic subject that you understand and enjoy.

◆ Interview people and turn your interviews into biographies. This exercise, though not an analysis of a text you are reading, nevertheless forces you to go outside yourself, to collect facts (proof), and to focus on the idea you are proving.

◆ Keep an informal literary journal about your personal response to the assigned reading.

◆ Write papers relating your experiences to the text you are studying.

◆ Write an original dialogue between characters and/or authors you have studied.

All these exercises will help you to gain the analytical skills necessary in academic writing while still allowing you to write out of your own experience.

LISTENING

When I hear the hypercritical quarreling about grammar . . . I see that they [grammarians] forget the first requisite and rule is that expression shall be vital and natural.

Henry David Thoreau

Since good writing (what Thoreau calls "vital and natural . . . expression") wants to be **heard**, **listen** to your words as you write. At first listen in your head; then, if you are lucky and the words keep coming, mouth them. Later, **read them aloud** so you can **hear** if they sound true and believable, or fake. The quality that makes a piece of writing want to be **heard** in a certain way is called **voice** or **tone of voice**. It begins in the early stages when you are really digging. If the voice in your paper sounds fake, you know you are fooling yourself, trying to say something you do not care about or do not believe. On the other hand, if the voice sounds strong and true, you know you are probably on the right track.

Notice the expression "the voice" and not "your voice." The voice you write in is not your speaking voice; it's the literary voice you have developed. Because the spoken voice sounds unnatural and is usually unclear on the written page, writers have to develop their natural literary voice. Listen to Joe Roland's voice as he argues that life is not just flesh and guts. In the poem he is discussing, "The Lull," by Molly Peacock, two characters have come across a dead possum.

No, Molly, we are not "Dreams, brains, fur / and guts."
We are dreams, memories, and fountains of emotions
that never quite give forth a burst that credits our

7

potential. What holds us together is not flesh but feeling. Feeling, and the learning to put up with one another's stench.

Joe Roland's voice **sounds** indignant, if not angry. It is the **arrangement** of the words, **not the words themselves**, that communicates this strong emotion. For instance, "No, Molly, we are not" directly contradicts the poet. Furthermore, Mr. Roland addresses the author by her first name, as if he knows Molly Peacock well. This presumed familiarity combined with the contradiction creates the vital and natural voice of an angry, righteous idealist who will not accept the poet's claim that life is only "dreams, brains, fur / and guts." Written in the middle ground between the academic and the personal, this paper compares the poet's response to a dead possum to a similar circumstance in Mr. Roland's life.

In the following example of personal writing, Lisa Arkfeld tells about her idea of home:

> I've never had a home in the conventional, capitalized sense of the word. Roots? What are they? 'Please list your permanent address.' What 'permanent address'?

What is the tone of voice in this passage? How does Ms. Arkfeld **arrange** her words to help create a vital tone of voice? Joe Roland's bare, bold "no" and his noun of direct address, "Molly," powerfully affect the passage's voice. Had Joe simply begun his sentence with "We are not. . . ," the voice would have lost its indignation. Look at Ms. Arkfeld's three, short interrogative sentences. How do those **arrangements of words** affect voice? What do they **sound** like? Merry? Lazy? Relaxed?

Now let us consider creating a voice in a purely academic paper, where you may not use informal language and sentence fragments, such as Lisa Arkfeld's sentence "Roots?" Listen to George Mack's voice as he discusses Charlotte, the protagonist in Anne Tyler's *Earthly Possessions*:

> There is a chance she never would have gone through with leaving, but she leaves because she is forced to. She does not offer any resistance. In a sense her kidnapper, Jake, represents the side of Charlotte that always wanted to leave. He lives freely, with no responsibilities. When he is finally faced with some responsibility – his girlfriend's having a baby and the thought of 'gold and avocado' curtains – he cringes. His realization that he cannot handle responsibility after his free floating life of crime and demolition derbies is similar to Charlotte's realization . . .

Unlike the two previous examples, no strong emotion intensifies the voice of this passage. How would you describe the author's voice? It is even, assured, and thus assuring – the voice of someone who knows what he thinks and has the facts to back up his ideas. George Mack understands Jake's irresponsibility and can express it concretely by mentioning the baby, the gold and avocado curtains, and the demolition derbies. This specific evidence and the apparent ease with which Mr. Mack employs it help create the passage's confident, natural, assured tone of voice.

Confidence also shows in the structure of this author's twenty-three word sentence beginning "When he is finally...." Note how Mr. Mack withholds "cringes," the main verb, until the very end. His sentence knows where it's going and thus it **sounds** confident and vital. The "vital and natural" expression in George Mack's writing is an intellectual vitality, the sound of someone who understands an **idea** and enjoys explaining it.

When Thoreau speaks of "hypercritical" grammarians quarreling, he means that writers must find

their own way of expressing thoughts **first** and **then** make sure they are writing clear, correct English. If you try to be correct in your first draft, your writing may not achieve the natural tone of voice that brings words alive. So let the words of your first drafts come quickly, **listen** to them, and read them aloud.

WRITING EXERCISES

1) Write 300–600 words in a strong voice of someone other than you. Choose a voice that you can hear in your head as you write, and try to write in such a way that your reader will say, "That is exactly what that person (or kind of person) sounds like!"

2) Write 300–600 words in your voice about a subject you know well. You could focus, for instance, on an issue you feel strongly about or a process that you enjoy and want others to know about. Again, think of engaging your readers with a realistic, convincing voice.

GOOD GROUND: SHOWING WHAT YOU MEAN

My task . . . is, by the power of the written word, to make you hear, to make you feel – it is, before all, to make you see.

Joseph Conrad

Though Joseph Conrad might have begun a book about writing with a chapter on description, most of the textbooks place description somewhere in the back, as if it is only decorative, something the writer adds on after the real work is finished, like the gingerbread on a Victorian house. Begin describing at the beginning, when you are digging out the words as fast as you can. It is easier for readers to remember a **thing** they have been **shown** than to remember an abstract idea, a concept. Though we never forget Macbeth's bloody hands, we find the abstract idea of guilt very forgettable. Shakespeare knew that abstractions wilt and die if tangible images (those red, dripping hands) do not take root in the reader's imagination.

In the passage below, Mike Raleigh uses imagery to bring a lacrosse player to life:

He played lacrosse with such a grace that he seemed to float just above the thick, green turf while all the others seemed to grind and cut through the field until it turned to dust.

No string of adjectives could have brought as much vitality into this passage as do its **nouns** and **verbs**. Nouns like **turf**, **field**, and **dust** carry the scene's sights, sounds and smells. Verbs like **float**, **grind**, and **cut** move the players in specific ways. We understand, therefore, what the author means by **grace** (an abstract word) because Mr. Raleigh has shown us graceful action and rooted it in the good ground of tangible (concrete) nouns and verbs.

Because nouns and verbs are the heart of language, use tangible ones as much as possible. If your idea for an academic paper isn't getting anywhere, if it is stuck in vague abstractions, look through the text you are writing about for a quotation full of concrete language. Then discuss why key words work well. Usually you will stumble on to a new idea in this process. In other words, instead of beginning with a rough, general idea – say, Macbeth's guilt – and going on to find specific examples for proof, pick out a specific passage about guilt and try to find ideas in it around which to build a paper. For instance, the passage about Macbeth's hands could lead to a discussion of how and why Shakespeare uses the image of blood throughout the play. This method of looking for general ideas in specific passages works well because in good writing each important passage contains nouns and verbs that support a general theme, such as the frightening power of evil suggested by bloody hands that cannot be washed clean. If you keep this fact in mind, you will write with strong nouns and verbs in the **first drafts of your papers**. Tacking on descriptive passages later is rarely productive.

If you are not convinced that nouns and verbs are the roots of strong writing, then consider what other parts of speech might qualify. Pronouns simply stand for nouns. Interjections are never central but only intensify what is central. (Wow, is she beautiful!) Conjunctions and prepositions connect and show important relationships between ideas. (Sarah jumped **over** (not **in**) the stream; John **or** (not **and**) Tom will drive.) Though properly used connectors **clarify** the relationship between your nouns and verbs, your nouns and verbs have to be clear in themselves.

What about adjectives and adverbs? What, for instance, does "thick, green" do for Mike Raleigh's "turf"? When we say **turf** instead of **field** or **ground**, don't we usually mean thick and green? The adjectives emphasize the depth and color of turf, making sure we see the image just as their author wants us to. Some would say that **turf** is enough, while others would say that **thick** and **green** are necessary. The question is of style. What do you think?

Most students use adjectives and adverbs too frequently, creating free-floating language, not rooted in the good ground of our five senses. Compare these abstract and rooted words.

Abstract	Rooted	
an old, famous, beautiful American tree that is now nearly extinct	an elm?	**VAGUE**
	a chestnut?	
a quick, dangerous turn	a swerve	
a long, prose story someone made up	a novel	
a small country just west of Spain	Portugal	

Notice that the abstract column is not only more vague than the rooted column, but also wordier.

Here are more examples of how nouns and verbs root language and save words:

Mr. Fenely, my sixth-grade band conductor, perched on his podium, glaring down at us like a vulture on some dying prey.

David Nute

VAGUE

Home is a doorjamb upon which has been recorded every centimeter of growth since the toddler age.

Lisa Arkfeld

Just after the Cross-County Parkway turns into Route 684, there is a very contemporary office building. I believe it belongs to the Aetna Corporation. . . . The sun reflects brightly off the cobalt blue, mirrored windows of the structure; and the parking lot's rows of cars are very evenly ordered, almost like a group of soldiers.

David Hart

What are the strongest nouns and verbs? What adjectives and adverbs work best? Note that some adjectives, like **cobalt**, are also nouns and that others, like **glaring** and **ordered** (participles), are also verbs. These adjectives, carrying their nounness and verbness along with them, are often stronger and livelier than adjectives that are only adjectives. What do you think of the **schoolgirl** friendship, the **summer** love, the **stolen** fruit, the **dying** horse, and the **red** Chevy? Note that these nouns and verbs used as adjectives strengthen the phrases.

In academic writing, the best way to **show** what you mean is to **blend** your words with the words of the text you are discussing. Note how Lee Scharges moves gracefully into a quotation that **shows** a character's determination to remain alone:

About twenty years later, after his father's death, the two are reunited by Catherine's ever-meddling Aunt Lavinia. Catherine, however, turns him away and 'picking up her morsel of fancy-work, [seats] herself with it again – for life, as it were.'

A writer less skilled than Lee Scharges might have handled the quotation this way:

. . .Catherine, however, turns him away. 'Picking up her morsel of fancy-work, [seats] herself with it again – for life, as it were.'

By not integrating the quoted words with his own sentence, this less skilled writer creates a choppy passage and what is called a **FLOATING QUOTATION** – one that is not part of the author's sentence but, rather, floats free. If you keep in mind that **all** quotations, no matter how long, are viewed grammatically as one word, you will realize that, in order not to be fragments, they must be used as some part of your sentence – subject, verb, direct object, whatever.

Here is a typical **FLOATING QUOTATION**: **Macbeth is courageous. "Give me my armor."** Correct this error by saying, **Macbeth, still courageous, says, "Give me my armor."** Now your quotation is part of the grammar of your sentence, the direct object of **says**.

Note now how Josh Scala's two quotations, like Lee Scharges', give us **things to see** and thus focus our imagination:

> The most outstanding metaphor in Dickinson's poem compares faith to a 'pierless bridge.' This bridge has no supports, which is impossible in real life, yet faith explains the impossible. By showing the soul as being 'rocked in arms of steel,' the poet [personifies] faith, the mother or generator of the soul.

Had Josh Scala not given us words that we can see like **pierless, arms, rocked, steel** and **support**, he would have left us unrooted and confused by abstractions like **faith** and **soul**.

These well-integrated quotations not only give the two passages substance and clarity, but also demonstrate a genuine familiarity with, if not admiration for, the text. A well-chosen, well-discussed passage, like a confident voice, will help convince your reader that you know what you are talking about.

And this passage does not have to be long. In fact,

FL QU a few words examined in depth are more effective than many words discussed superficially. Here, for example, is just one sentence by Jen Airoldi:

> The reader feels the bleakness of the 'gray and bare' jar and the wilderness surrounding its place 'upon a hill.'

By quoting two groups of three words from Wallace Stevens' poem "Anecdote of the Jar," by borrowing two other words that appeared in the poem (**jar** and **wilderness**), and by changing the forms of two others (**placed** becomes **place** and **surround** becomes **surrounding**), the author **blends** her language with Stevens'. In doing so, she assures us that she is comfortable with the language of the poem and that she understands the nature of the poem's **bleakness**, a very abstract word. Her reader is glad she did not simply say, "One feels the poem's bleakness." Instead, we **see** the bleakness of the "gray and bare" jar on its hill in the wilderness.

WRITING EXERCISES

1) Write 300–600 words of description about a subject you know well. Keep in mind that strong, specific nouns and verbs are the most effective tools of description. Also, don't forget that a confident, engaging voice convinces your readers that you know your subject.

2) In a piece of the same length, describe why a certain passage of poetry or fiction is effective. Use at least five well-chosen quotations. Avoid FL QU and unnecessarily long quotations.

GRAMMAR AND PUNCTUATION

*A knowledge of grammar is to the
writer as a knowledge of anatomy
is to the painter.*

Charles Lamb

As Charles Lamb suggests, the writer who recognizes and understands the powers and limitations of the various grammatical structures will be far more assured than the writer who must rely on his ear to decide questions of clarity, punctuation, and usage. In case your grammar is rusty, here is a review of the primary grammatical structures.

GRAMMAR REVIEW

G

PARTS OF SPEECH

NOUN – names a person, place, thing or idea; functions as a subject (Sub.), direct object (D.O.), indirect object (I.O.), object of the preposition (O.P.) and predicate nominative (P.N.)

> Ex. – Sally, Boston, freedom

PRONOUN – used in place of a noun

> Ex. – I, we, me, you, they, us, them, my, their, which, that, who, whose, whom, all, some, everyone, everybody, each

ADJECTIVE – modifies a noun or a pronoun

> Ex. – **mild** weather

VERB – expresses action or being

Transitive verbs take objects.

> Ex. – Ernest **drove** the truck.
> Ex. – Jim **walked** the dog.

Intransitive verbs express action but do not take objects.

> Ex. – Ernest **laughed**.
> Ex. – Ernest **ran**, but Jim **walked**.

Note that **to walk**, like many verbs, can be transitive or intransitive, depending on its use in the sentence.

Linking verbs link a subject to a P.A. or a P.N. They express thought but not action. The common linking verbs are all forms of **to be**, as well as **to feel**, **to loo**k, **to smell**, **to sound**, **to taste**, **to appear**, **to become**, and **to seem**.

> Ex. – Though the day **is** clear, the air **feels** cold.

ADVERB – modifies a verb, adjective, or another adverb and usually ends with *ly*

> Ex. – The sun shone **brilliantly**, and the time passed **too quickly**.

TWENTY-FIVE COMMON ADVERBS (that do not end in ly)			
almost	here	once	too
also	last	quite	twice
anyhow	late	rather	very
anyway	never	somehow	well
anywhere	not	someplace	
everywhere	now	somewhat	
far	often	there	

G

PREPOSITION – shows the relationship between a   **G**
  word and a noun or pronoun called the object of
  the preposition

> Ex. – **At** the end **of** the trail, Black Rock rises
> fifty feet **above** your head.

TWENTY-FIVE COMMON PREPOSITIONS			
above	between	inside	over
about	by	instead of	since
after	down	like	through
among	during	near	under
around	for	next to	to
at	from	of	
before	in	outside	

CONJUNCTION – joins words or groups of words

Coordinating conjunctions connect words, phrases,
and clauses of **equal** importance.

> Ex. – **for, and, nor, but, or, yet** (FANBOY)

Correlative conjunctions also connect words,
phrases, and clauses of **equal** importance.

> Ex. – **either** . . . **or, neither** . . . **nor, both** . . .
> **and, not only** . . . **but (also), whether** . . .
> **or, but** . . . **not**

Subordinating conjunctions begin dependent
clauses.

> Ex. – **because, before, if, while, when,**
> **although, since**

See *Dependent Clauses* (pages 24-27) for more
examples.

INTERJECTION – expresses emotion and has no grammatical connection with the rest of the sentence

> Ex. – **Well**, you finally showed up!
> Ex. – **Wow**, this view is beautiful!

THE PARTS OF A SENTENCE

This section reviews the ways we use the parts of speech to form complete thoughts.

SUBJECT – performs the primary action of the sentence or clause.

> Ex. – **Monica** threw the ball.

VERB or **SIMPLE PREDICATE** – describes the primary action or state of being in the sentence. The **predicate** is the verb and the words that modify and complement it.

> Ex. – Monica **threw** the ball.

DIRECT OBJECT – receives the action of a transitive verb.

> Ex. – Monica threw the **ball**.

INDIRECT OBJECT – precedes the direct object and tells who or what received the action. An indirect object either is or can be preceded by **to** or **for**.

> Ex. – Monica threw (to) **me** the ball.

OBJECTIVE COMPLEMENT – is a *noun* or an *adjective* that follows the direct object and that helps complete the meaning of a verb.

> Ex. – The players did not elect Osgood (D.O.) **captain** (O.C.), for no one considered him (D.O.) **qualified** (O.C.).
>
> Ex. – You make me (D.O.) **angry** (O.C.).

> This complement is used infrequently, for it follows only a few verbs such as **to name**, **to call**, **to consider**, **to make**, and **to elect**.

PREDICATE NOMINATIVE – follows a linking verb (p. 18) and restates the subject.

> Ex. – Monica is **captain**.

PREDICATE ADJECTIVE – follows a linking verb (p. 18) and modifies the subject.

> Ex. – Osgood is **isolated**.

APPOSITIVE – an appositive directly follows and restates a noun or a pronoun.

> Ex. – Monica, the **captain**, drinks root beer.

SUBJECT	APPOSITIVE	VERB OR SIMPLE PREDICATE	INDIRECT OBJECT	DIRECT OBJECT
Sally,	our friend,	sent	(to) us	the message

COMPOUND SUBJECT	COMPOUND PREDICATE	PREDICATE ADJECTIVE
Janet and Thomas	looked and felt	miserable.

	PREDICATE NOMINATIVE		OBJECTIVE COMPLEMENT
Since Monica is our	hero,	we have named her	captain.

VERBALS

Verbals are verbs used as other parts of speech.

GERUND – a verb used as a noun; always ends with *ing*; functions as a noun – subject (Sub.), direct object (D.O.), indirect object (I.O.), object of the preposition (Obj. of Prep.), object of a verbal (Obj. of Verbal) and predicate nominative (P.N.).

> Ex. – **Sleeping** mends the mind. (Sub.)
> Ex. – Janet loves **running**. (D.O.)
> Ex. – She is in the habit of **running**. (Obj. of Prep.)

PARTICIPLE – a verb used as an adjective, ends with *ing*, *ed* or with an irregular ending (beaten, swollen, grown).

> Ex. – The **hired** man held the **sleeping** cat.
> Ex. – Osgood's **tattered** and **worn** hat was thirty-years old.

INFINITIVE – a verb preceded by *to* and used as a noun, adjective, or adverb.

> Ex. – The stream wants **to run** (D.O.) where the hill begins **to fall**. (Adv.)

> Ex. – **To play baseball** (Sub.) seems **to be fun**. (P.A.)

> Note that **baseball** and **fun** are each part of infinitive phrases.

PHRASES

A phrase is a group of words that lacks a subject and/or a predicate and that acts as a unit.

VERBAL PHRASE – verbals that are modified and/or that take objects.

Gerund phrase

> Ex. – **Burying her hamster** helped Marybelle accept its death.

Participial phrase

> Ex. – **Dreaming of her lost summers**, Marybelle sipped a cherry Coke.

Infinitive phrase

> Ex. – Osgood loves **to oil his new baseball glove**.

PREPOSITIONAL PHRASES – a preposition always has an object.

> Ex. – The children sat **in the first row at the theater**.

APPOSITIVE PHRASES – an appositive directly follows and restates a noun or a pronoun.

> Ex. – Osgood, **the expert oiler**, lost his new glove.

> Ex. – Osgood, **the person who oiled his new glove eight times a day**, rarely caught a ball.

ABSOLUTE PHRASES – contain a subject and a participle or an infinitive; cannot stand alone as a sentence; do not serve as parts of a sentence or as modifiers.

> Ex. – **His glove lost in the woods**, Osgood looked miserable.

CLAUSES

A clause is a group of words that contains a subject and a predicate and that acts as a unit.

INDEPENDENT CLAUSE – a complete thought that can stand alone as a sentence.

> Ex. – **Marybelle leaped across Glen Brook**.

DEPENDENT CLAUSE – does not make sense alone.

Adjective clause (also called a relative clause) – modifies a noun or a pronoun and begins with the relative pronouns **which, who, whom, whose**, or **that**, and the relative adverbs **why, when** and **where**.

> Ex. – Marybelle, **who was already playing deep in center field**, caught the fly **that Jenny hit**.
> Ex. – Osgood, **whose ancient hat is turning green**, recalls the day **when his father gave it to him**.
> Ex. – Osgood's father, **whom everyone knows**, understands the reason **why old baseball hats are worth saving**.

Noun clause – acts as a noun (Sub., D.O., I.O., P.N., Appositive, Obj. of Prep., Obj. of Verbal) and often begins with these words: **how, that, who, whose, what, whoever, whomever, whatever, when, why, which, whether.**

Ex. – Tom told us **what we should wear** (D.O.), **where we should camp** (D.O.), and **how we would get there** (D.O.).

Ex. – **Whomever you choose** (Sub.) will be happy to play **where you wish** (Obj. of Infinitive).

Ex. – **Whether I should pick Marybelle or Jenny** (Sub.) is hard to decide.

Ex. – I know **why I can't decide** (D.O.).

Ex. – I'm afraid of **what the other person might think** (Obj. of Prep.).

Adverb clause – acts as an adverb and often begins with these subordinating conjunctions:

after	before	though
although	if	until
as	since	when
as though	so that	where
because	than	whether
		while

Ex. – **After Marybelle jumped Glen Brook**, she grabbed the ball.

Ex. – Marybelle hits better **than Jenny**. (Note that the verb **hits** is omitted. The adverb clause **than Jenny hits** modifies the adverb **better**.)

Ex. – We came inside **when the sun went down**.

25

G

Ex. – Elven, our center fielder, plays **where the grass grows high**.

Identifying Dependent Clauses

Since words like **that**, **when**, **which**, **why**, and **where** can begin more than one kind of dependent clause, you must understand the **function** of each clause – what the clause **does** within the sentence's structure. Keep these points in mind:

1. An adjective clause normally *follows a noun.*

   Ex. – The dog **that ate the bone** ran away.

2. Adverb clauses usually precede the subject or follow the complement (D.O., I.O., P.N., P.A.). Look, therefore, for adverb clauses at the beginnings and ends of sentences.

3. Like adverb clauses, noun clauses often appear at the beginnings and ends of sentences. A noun clause at the beginning of a sentence will probably function as the subject and, unlike an adverb clause, be followed by a verb. At the end of a sentence a noun clause functions as a complement (D.O., I.O., P.N., P.A.), completing the verb.

Now identify the adjective, adverb, and noun clauses below:

1. I know **that you love cities**.

2. You are the girl **who loves cities**.

3. I drove faster **so that I would not be late**.   **G**

4. Warm weather is the reason **why we moved south**.

5. I thank you for telling me **why you moved south**.

6. New York City is **where I want to be**.

7. Do you know the place **where I live**?

8. I remember the girl **whom we liked**.

9. I know the person of **whom you speak**.

10. **When the weather warms**, we'll play outside.

11. Remember the day **when we first met**?

ANSWERS:

(1) Noun clause – D.O. of **know**; (2) Adjective clause – modifies **girl**; (3) Adverb clause – modifies **faster**; (4) Adjective clause - modifies **reason**; (5) Noun clause – object of the gerund **telling**; (6) Noun clause – P.N. follows the linking verb **is** and restates the subject **New York City**; (7) Adjective clause – modifies **place**; (8) Adjective clause – modifies **girl**; (9) Noun clause – object of preposition **of**; (10) Adverb clause – modifies **will play**; (11) Adjective clause – modifies **day**

FOUR KINDS OF SENTENCE STRUCTURES

G   **SIMPLE** – one independent clause and no dependent clauses

    Ex. – Monica ran to second base.

COMPOUND – two or more independent clauses

    Ex. – Monica ran to second base, and Marybelle threw to third.

COMPLEX – an independent clause and one or more dependent clauses

    Ex. – As Monica ran to second base, Marybelle threw to third.

COMPOUND-COMPLEX – two or more independent clauses and one or more dependent clauses

    Ex. – As the umpire said, "Play on," Osgood found his glove behind the backstop, and Luther wildly pounded his fists on the ground.

FOUR KINDS OF SENTENCES

DECLARATIVE – makes a statement

    Ex. – The glove is green.

IMPERATIVE – gives a command or makes a request

    Ex. – Drop that vile glove, and please wash your hands.

INTERROGATIVE – asks a question

>   Ex. – How long was that glove behind the back-stop?

EXCLAMATORY – expresses strong feelings

>   Ex. – How lucky I am to have found my glove!

PUNCTUATION   P

Punctuation marks have four primary functions: **to end sentences**, **to introduce**, **to separate**, and **to set off**.

ENDING SENTENCES

1. Use a period to end declarative and imperative sentences.   .

>   Ex. – It's warm outside. Open the door.

2. Use a question mark to end interrogative sentences.   ?

>   Ex. – Why did Osgood oil his glove with olive oil?

3. Use an exclamation mark to end sentences expressing emotion.   !

>   Ex. – Osgood, you dope!

INTRODUCING

P   4. Place a comma **after introductory elements** in a sentence.

    a. *Adverbial clause*

       Ex. – When Osgood showed the team his glove, no one said much.

,   b. *Verbal phrase*

       Ex. – Sitting alone, Osgood began to cry.

    c. *Prepositional phrase* – when the comma is needed for clarity

       Ex. – From the other end of the long wooden bench, Monica heard Osgood.
       Ex. – In the evening they went to Elven Wood's house.

:   5. Use a colon **to introduce a list of appositives**, **a formal quotation**, and **a business letter**.

    a. list of appositives

       Ex. – Monica guesses that the forlorn sound is none of these things: a train whistle, a dying rabbit, or Marybelle's grandmother.

    Colons do **not** introduce a list of predicate nominatives or direct objects.

:   ERROR: Monica knew that the forlorn sound was: not a train whistle, a dying rabbit, or Marybelle's grandmother.

CORRECTION: Monica knew that the forlorn sound was not a train whistle, a dying rabbit, or Marybelle's grandmother.   **P**

b. formal quotation   **:**

> Ex. – All of a sudden Osgood rose and addressed his teammates: "I weep for my happiness in finding this great old glove."
> Ex. – Here are Osgood's words: "I weep for my happiness in finding this great old glove."

c. business letter

> Ex. – Dear Sir:
> Ex. – To whom it may concern:

SEPARATING

6. Separate independent clauses with a **comma and a coordinating conjunction** (for, and, nor, but, or, yet: FANBOY).   **,**

> Ex. – No one had actually realized that Osgood was crying, and only Monica paid attention to his announcement.

Independent clauses joined by a comma but with no coordinating conjunction (FANBOY) create a comma splice (CS).   **CS**

7. Use a **semicolon to separate independent clauses** not connected by a coordinating conjunction (FANBOY).   **;**

> Ex. – No one had noticed that Osgood was cry-

P ing; only Monica had paid attention to the address.

Conjunctive adverbs (such as **however, therefore, then, also, moreover**) joining main clauses must be preceded by a semicolon.

> Ex. – We played all day; then we went to the dance.
>
> Ex. – I love playing tennis; however, I hate having to take lessons.

; 8. Use a semicolon to separate independent clauses with internal punctuation.

> Ex. – No one had noticed that Osgood was crying; no one even looked up, I am sorry to report, except Monica, who wasn't even sure of what she had heard.

, 9. Separate **items in a series with commas** and use a comma before a coordinating conjunction.

> Ex. – Finally Osgood glanced down at Norton, Polly, Luther, and Monica.

; 10. Use a **semicolon** to separate **items in a series** when one or more of the items contain **internal punctuation**.

> Ex. – It was Marybelle – leaper of narrow water ways; Marybelle, dreamer of lost summers; Marybelle, cradler of sick and dying cats – who came running to Osgood's side.

11. Use a comma to separate a **series of adjectives** if their order does not affect the meaning of the phrase.

Ex. – the dusty, worn book
Ex. – the worn, dusty book
Ex. – the kind old lady
Ex. – the shy math teacher

Old kind lady would change the meaning of **kind old lady** because we consider **old lady** one idea modified by only one adjective, **kind**. Also, **the math shy teacher** obviously carries a different meaning than the **shy math teacher**.

12. Use a slant to indicate the end of a line of poetry.

> Ex. – Do you know the lines "I'm nobody! Who are you? / Are you nobody too?"

SETTING OFF

13. Pairs of commas **set off parenthetical expressions**, **appositives**, and **non-restrictive adjective clauses**.

a. Parenthetical expressions (**however, nevertheless, on the other hand, for example, moreover, for instance**)

> Ex. – Monica, however, got up and spoke to Osgood.
> Ex. – Luther, not to anyone's surprise, just stared at the ground.

b. Appositives and appositive phrases

> Ex. – Luther, the stone-faced prophet, noticed nothing.

P

Because **restrictive appositives** are essential to the sentence's meaning, they do not need to be set off with commas.

Ex. – The poet Homer, your friend Marybelle, the year 1953

Note that the appositives above tell which poet, which friend, and which year.

c. Non-restrictive adjective clauses

Ex. – Luther, who has written a book on the philosophy of bench-sitting, never says much.

Because **restrictive clauses are essential** to the sentence's meaning, **they do not need to be set off by commas**.

, ,

Ex. – The player who paid least attention to the game had ants in his glove.

The "who" clause (above) is essential (restrictive) because it identifies the player. (Player? Which player? The one **who paid least attention to the game**.)

, ,

14. Set off the second and **all** following items in an address or date.

Ex. – Marybelle married Osgood on September 13, 1953, in Rutherford, New Jersey, at the home of Dr. William Williams.

,

15. Set off words and phrases that introduce and explain quotations.

Ex. – Osgood asked, "May I play now?"
Ex. – Luther inquired, "What about the ants?"

16. Set off nouns of direct address.   **P**

    Ex. – Marybelle, may Osgood play?   **,**

17. Set off **yes** and **no**.   **,**

    Ex. – No, he may not play.

18. Use dashes to set off (a) a **series of appositives** or (b) an **appositive phrase with internal punctuation**.   **– –**

    Ex. – Luther – old shoe, old horse, constant companion, dark brooder on summer afternoons – why can't you be nice to Osgood?

    Ex. – Monica – the only one curious, bold, and crafty enough to catch and hold Luther's eyes – stepped solemnly toward Luther.

19. Set off incidental explanatory information in parentheses.   **( )**

    Ex. – Luther (he always wore rope sandals) considered his toes.

20. Use brackets to set off (a) **information within a quotation when the information is not part of the quotation** or (b) **explanations within parentheses**.   **[ ]**

    Ex. – At last Luther wrote on the pad he always carried, "I am a thousand years olde [o-l-d-e is Luther's spelling], and I am getting younger every day."

    Ex. – Monica turned toward the field (she was wearing her yellow blouse with the red polka dots [Monica was partial to polka dots] and   **[ ]**

P   her red shorts) and shouted, "Did you hear
            that?"

" "   21. Set off quotations in these ways:

            a. Place periods and commas **inside** end quotation
               marks.

            b. Place colons and semicolons **outside** end quota-
               tion marks.

            c. Place question marks and exclamation marks
               according to the sense of the sentence.

               Ex. – In his essay "Three Bags, One Plate and
                  One Plato," did Luther write, "Baseball is
                  Iowa; football is Tennessee"?

               Ex. – Marybelle asked, "If baseball is Iowa, then
                  is softball a state of the union or a state of the
                  mind?"

" "   Never use more than one end mark to conclude a
       sentence.

       ERROR: Did Marybelle ask, "If baseball is Iowa,
          then is softball a state of the union or a state of
          the mind?"?

       CORRECTION: Did Marybelle ask, "If baseball is
          Iowa, then is softball a state of the union or a
          state of the mind?"

            d. When writing dialogue, begin a new paragraph
               for each new speaker, no matter how little a
               speaker may say.

Ex. – "Luther, you're the smartest person I've ever known," said Marybelle.
"Thank you."
"I wish you were a better softball player."

e. When quoting more than two lines from a text, indent the passage on both margins, and do not use quotations; for your indentations have set the passage off for you. For an example, note the indented passage by Edward Abbey on pages 43-44.

f. Use quotation marks to indicate titles of essays, short stories, poems, song titles, one-act plays, titles of chapters, and articles. **Underline** (or italicize) titles of long works: novels (and all other books), plays, newspapers, magazines, films, and record albums.

Ex. – Luther's first book, *Baseball and the American Intellectual Tradition*, was praised in Willy Mays' essay "Why I Never Stop Reading."

22. Use ellipsis marks, three spaced periods (. . .), to show an interruption in quoted material. If ellipsis marks end your sentence, add a fourth period. Thoughtful use of ellipsis marks will help you rid quoted passages of words that do not further the point you are proving.

Ex. – Ray says, "We are mixing a cocktail of memories, and history, and love, and imagination."

W. P. Kinsella

Ex. – Ray speaks of ". . . mixing a cocktail of memories . . . and love. . . "

W. P. Kinsella

PRACTICE SENTENCES

P **Punctuation**

DIRECTIONS: Correct the error or errors in the following sentences, and in the space at the left write <u>the appropriate number(s) of the punctuation rule(s) that was(were) broken</u>. Place a *C* before sentences that are correct.

Most of the punctuation errors in sentences 1-15 focus on punctuation rules 1-12 on pages 29-33

_____ 1. When it rains this steadily in May the grass gets very green and the robin's chirps seem loud and shrill

_____ 2. Sitting inside here I can hardly keep my mind on my Spanish homework

_____ 3. After dinner I'll go outside for awhile

_____ 4. Do you ever take walks in the spring

_____ 5. For my big sister there is only one kind of walk long high speed ones.

_____ 6. Before one of those walks she quoted a line from an article in one of her nature magazines It's better to walk for ten minutes in the woods than to run an hour on a street

_____ 7. She says walking in the woods benefits three things your body your mind and your spirit

_____ 8. Three cheers for long walks says my sister

_____ 9. My brother says walking makes him tired hungry and grumpy

_____ 10. On a day like today when rainwater drips off **P**
every twig and bud it's hard for most people
to even imagine going outside they would
rather stay dry

_____ 11. Josh began the letter to his employer Dear
Mr Richards   I am writing to request a
transfer to Atlanta

_____ 12. Abe's letter to his friend began Dear Sam I
just asked my boss for a transfer however I
doubt that I'll receive one

_____ 13. We remembered the tent ground cloth and
cook kit but somehow we forgot sleeping
bags, which we had purchased especially for
the trip

_____ 14. The sly old man picked up his worn ancient
volume of Robert Frost's poetry and read
aloud this two-line poem Forgive O Lord my
little jokes on Thee And I'll forgive Thy great
big one on me

_____ 15. We were very happy we were very tired

Most of the punctuation errors in the sentences 16-40
focus on punctuation rules 13-22, pages 33-38.

_____ 16. The robin however   seemed to ignore the
cooper's hawk

_____ 17. In the spring we often see cooper's hawks
medium-sized raptors that prey on other
birds gliding through the trees near our
house

_____ 18. However many CDs he has in his room John
never seems to have enough

_____ 19. The writer Francis McCourt author of
Angela's Ashes gave a moving reading to a
gathering of English teachers and students

P

_____ 20. McCourt who was a high school teacher for most of his life knew his audience well

_____ 21. The climber who scrambled up the ledge the fastest was Sally from Seattle the city of misty sunsets

_____ 22. On September 4 1977 my family drove to Santa Barbara California to visit relatives

_____ 23. Alec asked Are you going to the prom

_____ 24. No I didn't hear him but did you hear Jean ask Are you still dating Maria

_____ 25. George shut the door please

_____ 26. White spring wildflowers especially blood-root Dutchman's breeches saxifrage and Painted Trillium abound in the New England woods

_____ 27. Painted Trillium we always find them about halfway up the mountain are the most beautiful spring wildflower in this part of the state

_____ 28. Coleridge's poem The Rime we usually spell the word r-h-y-m-e of the Ancient Mariner still moves us powerfully

_____ 29. John's new mountain bike it cost $1,543.95 his parents buy him anything he wants encountered a sturdy young oak tree about six inches in diameter the tree looks fine

_____ 30. After the accident John said rudely to his mother Aren't you glad you have insurance

_____ 31. His mother who wasn't pleased said I'm glad you have a summer job to pay for the repair if it can be repaired

_____ 32. Leslie told us don't forget your game shoes she is good about reminding everyone about details

_____ 33. Get ready to go his roommate said to Bill who is often late to class

_____ 34. I heard Bill mutter to himself why should I rush

_____ 35. I have to go to play practice after dinner Al announced to Tom and Lucy And I have a literary society meeting Tom said well I guess I'll just go for a walk all by myself said Lucy sweetly

_____ 36. My mother loves to quote these four lines from Emily Dickinson This is my Letter to the world, That never wrote to me – The simple news that nature told, With tender majesty

_____ 37. The Lottery was the most popular short story we read last year, There Eyes Were Watching God was the favorite novel, and A Midsummer's Night Dream ranked as the best play

_____ 38. The New York Times, Redbook and Gourmet all ran articles entitled Food for Fun

_____ 39. Everyone in the class memorized the famous soliloquy from Shakespeare's Hamlet To be – the question [the author of this sentence has used a dash to indicate that eight words are left out.]

_____ 40. The bluebirds found the box we built the sparrow found it first

SHAPING PAPERS

The writer must to some extent inspire himself. Most of his sentences may at first be dead in his essay, but when they are all arranged, some life and color will be reflected on them from the mature and successful lines . . . and he will be able to eke out their slumbering sense. . . .

Henry David Thoreau

To shape your free writing is "to eke out" the "slumbering sense" of your best lines by rearranging words and throwing out what does not fit your purposes. So far you have worked with a rough idea, a hunch. Here are some ways to clarify a rough idea and focus your paper upon it.

SHAPING PERSONAL WRITING

POINT OF VIEW

If you are writing an autobiographical paper or a short story, you have probably done your free writing in the first person. Question why you are telling the story yourself and not having another narrator tell it. If the event you describe involves you directly, perhaps you should shift the **point of view** away from you, the central character, to a secondary character or to an omniscient narrator. Selecting a personal paper's narrator, its **point of view**, affects your paper's shape and focus.

PT V

If you write, for instance, about the time you ran through a sliding glass door when you were six, you

42

will probably begin writing as an older person looking back on the event. This **point of view** will distance your reader from the action. He or she knows, after all, that you survived and are looking at the event in retrospect. What if, on the other hand, you tell the story in the voice of the six-year-old you used to be, or of your mother who wasn't there at the time, or of the babysitter who was, or of the doctor who sewed the ten stitches in your forehead? As you examine the merits of each point of view, you will learn something about your story's purpose. Remember, because readers aren't going to care about your accident unless they can relate to it, you'll have to bring your tale alive. Perhaps the words of a six-year-old would, in their innocence, be amusing and powerful. Perhaps the babysitter's point of view would move your audience, many of whom may have baby-sat. Perhaps, by having your mother tell the story, you would discover that your real interest is how your mother felt when she read the babysitter's note saying you were at the hospital having your scalp sewn up. Rewriting a story in a new point of view is to a writer what taking a picture from a new position is to a photographer: both of you are looking for just the right angle.

PT V

This experimentation with point of view also helps writers develop a voice, for when speaking in the voices of others, we think and say things we would not normally think of. In many ways, we write in costume; and like anyone in costume, we enjoy the freedom of not being the person everyone thinks we are. Edward Abbey, a novelist and essayist, says this of the narrator he uses in his essays:

> The Edward Abbey of my own books, for example, bears only the dimmest resemblance to the shy, timid, reclusive, rather dapper little gentleman who, always cor-

rectly attired for his labors in coat and tie and starched detachable cuffs, sits down each night for precisely four hours to type out the further adventures of that arrogant, blustering, macho fraud who counterfeits his name.

Who is the real Edward Abbey – the narrator of his essays or the narrator of this quoted sentence? Probably neither. The point is that Edward Abbey the man has learned that he can write his essays most effectively through the voice of Edward Abbey the literary character. Try this trick; it is like acting a part in a play.

ORDERING EVENTS

Point of view raises the question of the order of events, for each narrator experiences a narrative (story) differently. The mother, for instance, would begin her story with finding the sitter's note, while a detached narrator (like the child looking back years later) might relate the events in a clear, chronological order. The beauty of telling stories, true or fictional, is that the chronological order is always there to use. But chronology can be boring if there aren't surprises along the way, complications that will hold your readers' interest. For instance, the flight of Malcolm and the escape of Fleance complicate Macbeth's plans and keep the reader wondering what will happen next.

Rather than dragging the reader through each adventure in the order that it occurred, Homer begins *The Odyssey* in the middle of things (in medias res). He then flashes back to the beginning, catches up to the middle, and finishes chronologically. To decide how to order the events of a story, question your purpose. Is it to reveal character, to surprise or shock, to develop a theme, or a combination of these? Like the question of point of view, the question of order implies purpose. What do you want your point of view to do for your paper? How will the order of events affect the way your reader understands your point?

WRITING EXERCISE

Write **three** short pieces, 150–300 words in length describing an event or process from **three different points of view**. Have fun; use your imagination; take advantage of the potential irony and humor that multiple narration can create. Keep in mind that different narrators are apt to order their ideas differently.

SHAPING ACADEMIC WRITING

DEVELOPING A THESIS

THESIS

Unlike personal papers, academic papers require that you, the student, narrate and that you organize your material according to the logic of your argument. To discover the purpose of an academic paper is to discover exactly what you want your argument to prove. Ask yourself these questions about the idea you've been trying to develop in your free writing.

◆ **Do I have an argument to prove?**

If so, try writing it out in a SENTENCE. Arguments are sentences, not just phrases. Some **thing** (subject) must **happen** (verb).

Here is a non-argument: **Evil in *Macbeth*.** This idea has no action.

Give it a verb: **Evil is a theme in *Macbeth*.** Now you have to **prove** that evil is a theme in the play.

THESIS

◆ **Is my argument too broad?**
Yes. Because evil permeates *Macbeth*, you'll be able to find it practically anywhere, and your paper will be too broad for you to show a real familiarity with the text. Your teacher, who wants to find out if you understand the significant details of plot and the fine points of character, will not be impressed by an argument based exclusively on relatively obvious facts of plot, such as Macbeth's murder of Duncan. Look for an argument that will investigate beyond the obvious facts of plot to make **inferences** – conclusions you have drawn from facts. Here is another, more specific argument about evil: **The three witches are the primary source of evil in *Macbeth*.** Now you have narrowed your focus to the three witches.

◆ **What am I disproving?**
Since all sound arguments must argue **against** as well as **for**, you will have to **dis**prove points that appear to contradict or weaken your case. For instance, the paper about the three witches could begin this way: **Though the main events of the play appear to be initiated by Lady Macbeth and Macbeth, the three witches control the play's primary action.** Now you have something to **dis**prove – that though Macbeth and Lady Macbeth commit evil deeds, they are not the source of evil. You have given your paper an antagonistic force; and once you have defeated this force, proven

46

it invalid, you will have strengthened the validity of
your main argument.

LOGICAL ORGANIZATION

◆ **How will I organize my argument?**
Most teachers like to see your main idea in your
first paragraph so that, knowing from the start just
what you intend to prove, they can follow your argument carefully. More important than where you
place your main idea – also called a **thesis state-
ment** – is that you create a clear, logical **line of**   **LOGIC**
thought from sentence to sentence and paragraph
to paragraph (>). Here is a rough line of thought.   **>**

1 - Introduce and state your main idea (**thesis**)
about how the witches control Macbeth's primary
action.

2 - Show how Lady Macbeth reacts to Macbeth's letter, which is in itself a reaction to the witches'
prophecies. Quote Lady Macbeth and discuss
your quotations.

3 - Show that though the murder of Duncan is a
response to Lady Macbeth's urgings and to
Macbeth's ambition (quote to prove this ambition), the witches' prophecy has encouraged this
ambition and has prompted the letter.

4 - Discuss the finer points of Macbeth's character –
his bravery in battle, his reputation as a loyal
thane, and his susceptibility (in contrast to
Banquo) to the witches' prophecies.

5 - Return to plot and observe how the second set of
prophecies propels the play to its conclusion.

6 - Conclude **not** with a boring rehash of your main

argument, but with what you have proven – that **because** the witches are the play's source of action and **because** the witches personify evil, Shakespeare's play frightens us by suggesting that evil is a real and powerful force.

These six points have begun to organize your free writing into a logical **line of thought**. Perhaps you will find that in this stage you will be able to modify and rearrange ideas and examples from your free writing, but most likely you will discover some points that you have not yet considered. If so, you are still learning about the text.

Now write out your summary as a first draft of your paper, and pay attention to these elements of organization:

THE BEGINNING

Think not only of stating your thesis in the first paragraph but also of writing an **engaging** opening sentence that will begin your paper strongly. Your thesis itself, or a preliminary form of it, can also serve as your opener. You could write, for instance, **Though they appear in only three short scenes, the three witches in Shakespeare's *Macbeth* control the central action of the play**. This opener states the title and author of the work being considered, announces the paper's basic thesis, and withholds for later in the paragraph the points that the writer must disprove.

If you can introduce your paper and your thesis in one sentence, **do not write a one-sentence paragraph**. Instead, simply merge your sentence with the first point you intend to discuss, thus avoiding a one sentence paragraph.

THE INTERNAL PARAGRAPHS ¶

In academic writing, paragraphs are rarely shorter than three or four sentences because they must provide a transition from the previous paragraph, state a general idea called a **topic**, prove the idea with specific evidence, and then conclude. Most internal paragraphs, therefore, are miniature essays with their own general points to prove. If a paragraph or a whole paper offers generalities without sufficient supporting evidence (**proof**), the reader will not be convinced. (In a longer paper, we might need a paragraph of generalities to help the reader follow the line of a long argument: "As we have seen thus far, . . .") On the other hand, if the paper offers a great deal of textual proof without stopping regularly to state the generality being proven, the reader will become confused and disengaged. Successful papers move paragraph by paragraph, from generality to specific and back to generality.

PROOF

THE TRANSITIONS

As you write out your summary in paragraph form, you'll have to clarify the relationship between each paragraph so that your **line of thought** will remain, perhaps not straight, but always clear. For instance, point four, in order to treat Macbeth's character, puts aside the discussion of how the witches affect the plot's action. This interlude proves the essential point that the witches alter Macbeth's char-

TRANS

acter and gives the reader a rest from the review of important but obvious facts of plot. The conclusion of this paragraph and the beginning of the next must put the reader back on the track of the witches' influence upon plot. Look over the six summarized points and think of transitions that will take the reader from one point to the next.

AVOIDING GROCERY LISTS

G L

Transitions that do not develop ideas but simply add on more are called "**grocery list**" transitions. If you find yourself beginning paragraphs with "another reason" and "also," you are not **building** on the previous paragraph; you are just piling on more ideas. Grocery lists often begin with main ideas like this: Three forces destroy Macbeth – his ambition, his wife, and the three witches. The internal paragraphs are apt to sound like "The first reason is . . . ," "The second reason is . . . ," "The third reason is . . . " Not very interesting! The student could improve this paper by shaping those three points into a logical order and by using transitions that make the order explicit. Below are three transitional sentences.

– Before blaming the fall of Macbeth entirely upon outside forces, one should consider his powerful ambition.

– Lady Macbeth feeds her husband's ambition.

– The three witches, however, appear to be the greatest force behind Macbeth's tragic fall.

Now this paper **develops** by **building** one idea upon another. When it reaches its conclusion, it will have traveled a bit; and its author may have learned enough to end with an interesting thought.

THE ENDING

Because introductions set up endings, papers that have no clear point to prove cannot be concluded gracefully. Usually papers like this just stop. For instance, **Evil in Macbeth** would be hard to end because it would just list examples of evil, and there can always be one more item on a grocery list. Even though you may think you have mentioned every example of evil in **Macbeth**, your reader will not know you are at the end of your list until you get there and say, "And the final example. . . . " Your paper will be ready to end not because you have concluded your argument, but because you've **said** you are finished.

On the other hand, a logically developing essay, having proceeded step by step from paragraph to paragraph, will conclude itself when it has proven your point. You will not have to say something like "And so one can easily see. . . " or "Thus, it is obviously clear that. . . " When you find yourself having to use stilted phrases like these, check your main argument. Is it there? Have you proven it logically, step by step?

LOGIC

As you check your logic, look for these two common problems:

◆ Unqualified generalization – generalizes with sweeping statements

LOGIC

Ex. – **Everyone** knows Lady Macbeth helped Macbeth.

Ex. – **No one** likes to hike.

Ex. – Frederic Henry **never** is frightened.

To avoid unqualified generalizations, use qualifiers like these: **often**, **usually**, **rarely**, **in many cases**, **frequently**.

◆ Hasty generalization – makes a broad generalization from too little evidence

Ex. – *Macbeth* is a violent play; therefore, all of Shakespeare's plays are violent.

Ex. – Because I can't play football, I probably can't play any outdoor sport.

WRITING EXERCISES

1) Using as your text a novel or short story you are reading in class, develop a thesis using the three questions explained under "Developing a Thesis": Do I have an argument to prove? Is my argument too broad? What am I disproving? When you present your thesis, be prepared to explain how you have dealt with each question.

2) Write a logically organized outline or summary that presents the main points of your paper.

3) Write the first draft of your paper. Underline the thesis, the topic sentences of the internal paragraphs, your transitions, and the main idea of your concluding paragraph.

4) Edit, revise, and re-revise your first draft, keeping in mind that all good writing is rewriting.

5) Write your final draft.

HOW TO WRITE ACADEMIC ESSAYS ABOUT POETRY

Since each word of a poem carries a great deal of meaning and since this meaning is not only denotative (what a word literally means) but also connotative (what a word suggests) and aural (the music a word helps to make), you will have to discuss specific words and phrases **in depth**. Long quotations followed by brief discussions suggest a superficial analysis. Here are some ways to be sure that your essays make useful observations about the ways that poems work:

1) Explain the poem's literal level – what physically happens, even if it is impossible in real life. When Emily Dickinson says below, "Hope is a thing with feathers," she means just that.

254

"Hope" is a thing with feathers –
That perches in the soul –
And sings the tune without the words –
And never stops – at all –

And sweetest – in the Gale – is heard
And sore must be the storm –
That could abash the little Bird
That kept so many warm –

I've heard it in the chillest land –
And on the strangest Sea –
Yet, never, in Extremity,
It asked a crumb – of Me.

Remember, we must give ourselves over to the world of the poem, accept it as it is, and ask questions later – even though we know, for instance, that abstract ideas (like hope) do not have physical properties (like feathers). Since the poet always means what he or she says, we never have to hunt for "hidden meanings."

2) Ask yourself what appeals to you most about the poem (if nothing appeals, write about another poem); then identify the device(s) that create(s) that appeal. **Always** remind yourself that if theme were all, the poet could have written a sentence of prose. For instance, if Emily Dickinson had wanted to say no more than that hope is always with us, no matter how hard life gets, why did she bother to write four closely rhymed and metered quatrains of poetry? There must be something in the **way** Emily Dickinson constructed her poem that makes the theme appealing. You must discover and articulate that **way**, that **how**.

3) Some observations about mediocre, good, and excellent poetry papers:

Mediocre papers never advance beyond a discussion of theme. To say that hope is always with us, even in times of trouble is not "wrong," for the poem's bird does sing most sweetly in the gale. But there is much more to say about **how** the poet conveys her meaning, about the **way** the poem affects the reader.

Good papers say that the poem contains a central metaphor (hope is a bird), which the poet extends by having the bird survive a "gale" and the "chillest lands." Then these good papers may go on to identify other poetic devices such as the ABAB rhyme scheme, the alliteration in "strangest sea," the interesting off rhyme of "soul" and "all," and the strong visual imagery in words like "feathers," "perches," and "crumb." It is clear that the authors of these papers can recognize poetic devices, but it is also clear that the authors cannot explain how the devices actually make the poem effective. Usually these student writers resort to cheerleading: "the vivid images in this poem are extremely effective" . . . "Emily Dickinson uses off rhyme brilliantly" . . ."only a poet as great as Dickinson could have extended her central metaphor, hope is a bird, for twelve magnificent lines." . . . Though these statements may sound impressive, none of them proves that their author understands how each technique actually works in this poem. We know only that the student can recognize poetic devices and that he or she thinks that if Emily Dickinson uses them, it is safe to say that she uses them brilliantly.

Some students who recognize that they must do more than state that the poet uses a certain device but who do not know what to say about **how** that device functions in the poem, stray from the text in search of something to say:

> As we all know, birds are very hopeful little fellows. They come back to the same nest each year, usually, even though the tree might have been cut down

for a development. This sad situation occurred right next door to me . . . .

Stick closely to the text, making only **careful inferences that fit into the context of the whole poem**. Man's encroachment upon nature has nothing to do with Dickinson's meditation upon the nature of hope.

The best papers explain the poem's literal level, state the theme, identify the poetic devices that make significant contributions to theme, and (most important) explain how the poetic devices make the poem moving. Note these two examples:

> One pictures a chickadee or a sparrow clinging to a branch in a February storm.

> Had Emily Dickinson said in her first line, 'Hope is a bird,' she would not have involved the reader's visual and tactile senses as she does with the phrase, 'a thing with feathers.' We understand that the 'thing' is a bird; we see the feathers; and we wonder what kind of a bird this is. Later the poet shows us her 'little bird.'

Note that the two examples above testify to their author's interest in and appreciation of the poem. Because the student has explained how the metaphor in the first line has affected his imagination, it would be superfluous for him to say that he likes the poem or that Emily Dickinson is a fine poet. Note also that the first example, while illustrating the poem's power to evoke an image in the reader's imagination, does not distort the poem by going too far, as does the example of the development next door. Also, this first example does not fall into the common trap of saying that the "little bird" **is** a chickadee or a sparrow. This wise student knows that because a poem means what it says, the "little bird" can never be any more than that, but it can and does **suggest** a chickadee or sparrow to an American reader.

The second example could have simply read, "Hope is a thing with feathers is a very effective metaphor"; but, instead, it shows us **how** the metaphor involves our mind and our senses. In other words, this second example examines how a poetic device functions to help the poem affect the reader.

WRITING EXERCISE

Using as your text a poem you are reading in class, employ the following process to write a 300–to 600-word academic essay:

1) Write out the poem's literal meaning in the form of a paraphrase.

2) Write some notes on what aspect of the poem appeals to you most. Say **why** you like specific words, phrases, lines, and poetic devices.

3) Now write an essay that
   (a) presents a **thesis** which states directly why the poem is effective;
   (b) reviews the poem's **literal meaning**;
   (c) identifies **significant elements**, such as the speaker's tone of voice, theme, sound devices, and figurative language;
   (d) explains **how** these elements contribute to the poem's effectiveness.

PREPARING FOR STANDARDIZED EXAMINATIONS

The next two parts of *The Portable Writer*, "Shaping Sentences" and "Being Correct," contain most of the material covered on standardized examinations such as the A.C.T., the expanded PSAT/NMSQT, and the S.A.T. II. As you study these chapters thoroughly, remind yourself that because test makers know what "sounds right" to most students and what does not, you cannot trust your ear to tell you if a passage is correct. Instead, **you must know the rule**. For instance, "between you and I" sounds correct to many people; but since the object of the preposition *between* must be in the objective case, "between you and me" (not *I*) is correct. Note, therefore, the rules in the next two parts and pay particular attention to right words that sound wrong and to wrong words that sound right.

SHAPING SENTENCES

> *All I know about grammar is its infinite power. To shape the structure of a sentence alters the meaning of that sentence as definitely and inflexibly as the position of a camera alters the meaning of the object photographed. Many people know about camera angles now, but not many know about sentences.*
>
> Joan Didion

A sentence is more than "a complete thought"; it's an **action**: some **thing** (subject) **happens** (verb). You, the writer, use grammar to shape and direct your reader's response to this action.

When Robert Frost wrote that to write is to go "a-sentencing," he suggested that a sturdy sentence, like wild game, is elusive and must be hunted down. Here is a rewrite of Robert Frost's famous first lines from "Stopping by Woods on a Snowy Evening":

> You thought it was known by you whose woods these were, though his house was in the village.

This is the original:

> Whose woods these are I think I know.
> His house is in the village though.

Although the original and the rewrite have different meanings, their nouns and verbs are essentially the same. The differences come from the **angles** from which the nouns and verbs appear; for the rewrite has changed the tense, voice, person, and grammatical emphasis. Here are ways you can use grammar to shape the actions of your sentences:

PERSON, AUDIENCE, AND
MORE POINT OF VIEW

When a writer decides who will narrate a piece of writing, he is really deciding the **point** (or angle) from which his reader will **view** the piece. For instance, though Frost could have said, "**we** think we know," "**they** think they know," or "**you** think you know," he wanted to center the sentence's action on his narrator, his "I." How do you think other points of view would have altered the meaning of the lines?

As we have discussed, academic papers – unlike all forms of personal writing, including poems – require that the narrator be objective and out of the way. When Robert Frost says later in the poem, "I have promises to keep/And miles to go before I sleep," he **wants** his reader to identify with the speaker. On the other hand, when you argue logically and concretely that the three witches control the action of *Macbeth*, an "I think" **distracts** the reader and **weakens** your argument's objectivity.

Person involves your audience as well as your narrator. Think about how the following phrases affect the way your reader relates to your narrator:

– You know how easy it is to forget an aunt's birthday.

– One can easily forget . . . !

– We know how easy it is to forget. . . .

– The reader knows how easy it is to forget. . . .

– It's easy for me to forget. . . .

You and **we** are familiar, while **one** and **the reader** keep a formal distance, and **It's easy for me** ignores the reader. In academic papers, you will want this formal distance between your narrator and your audience, but in personal papers, you may need to draw your reader into your essay or story.

COMMON PROBLEMS WITH PERSON **PERS**

a. Do not use the first person in literary analysis.

b. Avoid shifts of person.

ERROR: If **one** is interested in oiling baseball gloves, **you** should talk to Osgood.

CORRECTION: If **one** is interested in oiling baseball gloves, **he** or **she** should talk to Osgood.

c. Avoid using **you** impersonally.

ERROR: **You** come to dislike Macbeth.

CORRECTION: **One** comes to dislike Macbeth.

d. Use **you** to refer to a specific person.

Ex. – Marybelle, **you** will play shortstop.

In informal English, you may address the reader personally as "you." Do not, however, use **you** in an academic essay. Rely not upon being personal, but upon the strength of your argument.

VERB TENSE

The past tense completes action – making it safe, finished, historic, and sometimes even nostalgic. The future tense also moves action a safe distance away. A prophecy of future action can be intriguing, even engrossing, but the reader knows that it has not happened. On the other hand, the present tense happens before our eyes.

For evidence of the present tense's power, ask yourself why students often shy away from it. Unless reminded, inexperienced writers discuss literature in the past tense – even though they know that Holden Caulfield, Macbeth, and Frederic Henry are as **present** on the page now as they have ever been. Inexperienced writers also set personal papers safely in the past, rather than giving the reader a close-up of the action. When concluding arguments, these writers usually say that the reader **will** see or **has seen** or **can** see, but rarely do they say that the reader **sees**. Why? Because the present tense is **now**; it's inescapable, and thus it makes the less confident writer uneasy.

Some writers begin in the past and then bring the action to the present, thus easing the reader into the starkness of the present. Some writers treat the past or the future as if it were present. Science fiction writers and historical novelists usually tell their stories in the present tense, thus putting what is safely distant right before one's eyes. Similarly, historians make their subject vital by using the **historical present**.

All the tenses have their particular uses. To use them appropriately, keep the following points in mind:

a. Write academic essays in the present tense.

b. Do not shift tenses arbitrarily.

ERROR: At the beginning of the novel, Frederic Henry **did** not **know** Catherine, but eventually he **falls** in love with her.

CORRECTION: At the beginning of the novel, Frederic Henry **does** not **know** Catherine, but eventually he **falls** in love with her.

c. The progressive form of the verb (I am walking, was walking, have been walking, had been walking, will have been walking) describes **action in progress** and is rarely useful in an academic essay.

WEAK: Shakespeare is using the image of blood.

STRONG: Shakespeare uses the image of blood.

d. Use the past perfect tense (I had walked, you had walked, etc.) to express **action completed in the past before some other action**.

ERROR: Once Monica caught Luther's attention, he began to philosophize.

CORRECTION: Once Monica **had caught** Luther's attention, he began to philosophize.

PRACTICE SENTENCES

VT **Verb Tense**

DIRECTIONS: On a separate piece of paper, write out the following sentences correctly. If the sentence contains no errors, simply write a *C*.

1. Just as the game seemed lost, Sam ties it up with two quick goals.
2. My science teacher showed me that trees grew annual rings in the trunk.
3. Ptolemy taught that the sun would revolve around the earth.
4. In Wu Cheng'en's classic Chinese novel *Journey to the West*, Monkey, the central character, often behaved like Odysseus.
5. Everyone spoke by the time I arrived.
6. Everyone had spoken by the time I had arrived.
7. When the end of study hall came, my work was not finished.
8. My brother, who hoped to make the varsity by his senior year, actually started on the varsity by the end of his junior year.
9. Dan would like to join the Navy, but he failed the physical.
10. Having hiked the Appalachian Trail in early spring, we spot many wildflowers.
11. In *A Lost Lady* Willa Cather is developing a conflict between idealism and reality.
12. Do you think that Hemingway is creating a weak character in Catharine?
13. Fleur, the main character in *Tracks* by Louise Erdrick, was cutting tree trunks halfway through, so that the next windstorm blew them over.
14. By the time the class ended I took ten pages of notes.
15. Back in mid-March, before most spring wildflowers finally had bloom, I looked for them on the north bank of the pond.

VOICE

The **active voice** makes the doer of action the subject and the receiver of action the direct object.

Ex. – Osgood oiled his glove.

The **passive voice** turns a sentence around, making the direct object the subject and either changing the original subject to an object of a preposition or removing it from your sentence. **Avoid the weak passive**. **WP**

WEAK PASSIVE: The glove is oiled by Osgood.

or

The glove is oiled.

If the object of action concerns you more that the doer of action, then use the passive voice.

USEFUL PASSIVE: Luther's books are widely read.

Because this sentence needn't be concerned with **who** reads Luther's books, the passive works well, for it emphasizes Luther's books, the real subject of our concern.

Note that the passive voice, which comes in all tenses (was read, is read, will be read, had been read, has been read, will have been read), **should not be confused with the past tense**.

PRACTICE SENTENCES

Weak Passive

DIRECTIONS: On a separate piece of paper, write out the following sentences correctly. If the sentence contains no errors, simply write a *C*.

1. A new sled was wanted by Herman for Christmas.
2. It was decided to require bicyclists to wear helmets.
3. After their arrival, visiting families will be given a tour of the campus.
4. With less than a minute left in the game, the winning goal was scored by Alice.
5. Cucumber sandwiches and fresh scones were served at the tea party.
6. Uniforms will be handed out at the gym one hour before the game.
7. Shakespeare's *Othello* is portraying jealousy and its damaging effects.
8. To reach Great Barrington, either Route 7 or Route 41 may be taken.
9. It was raining all afternoon.
10. Being tired from his performance, the actor lay down on the couch in the green room.

SUB   # SUBORDINATION

Subordination is emphasis – expressing main ideas in independent clauses and subordinate (less important) ideas in dependent clauses, phrases, and single words. The emphasis of Robert Frost's two lines (page 59) changes when **though** is moved from the end of the second sentence to the beginning, where it

subordinates the second sentence into an adverbial   **SUB**
clause modifying "know." "His house is in the village
though" became "though his house is in the village."
Joan Didion would call the shifting of **though** a cru-
cial change of angle. How does this shifting of one
word change Frost's meaning?

Here is a choppy passage that, unlike Frost's sentences, needs subordination:

> CHOPPY: Luther had long black hair. He tied
> on a bandanna. It was red. He'd made him-
> self look like an Apache.

> SUBORDINATED: The red bandanna tied
> around his long black hair made Luther
> look like an Apache.

Below is an exaggerated form of a stringy compound sentence. Most compound sentences can be
rewritten as a complex or simple sentence.

> CHOPPY: *Macbeth* is a tragedy, and it was writ-
> ten by William Shakespeare, and it is a vio-
> lent play, but it attracts large audiences.

> SUBORDINATED: William Shakespeare's
> *Macbeth*, though a violent play, attracts
> large audiences.

This moving of words from one grammatical structure
to another clarifies thought, smoothes out choppy sentences, and shakes off unnecessary words.

PRACTICE SENTENCES

SUB   **Subordination**

DIRECTIONS: On a separate piece of paper, write out the following sentences correctly. If the sentence contains no errors, simply write a *C*.

1. I was driving home from my new job, heading northward on Route 71, when my car overheated.
2. The coach noticed that I was holding the hockey stick awkwardly and asked if I was left-handed or right-handed.
3. I mowed for three hours. I finally finished the lawn.
4. The group packed food and cooking gear. They packed clothing, sleeping bags, and other personal equipment. They also took a tent.
5. Picasso is my favorite painter. I love the variety of his work.
6. Our lacrosse coach tells us to bend at the waist when we are scooping, always step into the ball, and she likes us to cradle the ball hard.
7. I e-mailed my sister. She lives in Ireland.
8. We walked outside. We heard a cardinal singing.
9. He is hot-tempered. I enjoy his company.
10. I exercised regularly for a month, and I made the lacrosse team for the first time in my high-school career.
11. Larry is an A student. He received a C in the course. He had been ill for two weeks.
12. In New England no one expects spring to come early. We were amazed to have a week of hot weather in early April.
13. Harry is a fine athlete. We are happy to have him on our team.
14. The fish swam near our boat. The fish seemed a

yard long. It was orange. I think it was a carp. We were in China. It was last March.

15. It is late May. The temperature is only forty degrees. The wind is blowing hard from the north. The lilacs aren't even out yet. It's cloudy. I think it will rain soon. I hate this weather.

PARALLELISM

Parallelism expresses parallel ideas in parallel grammatical structure. Like subordination, parallelism structures the grammar of a sentence to complement its meaning. Though, strictly speaking, a compound sentence puts two or more independent clauses in a parallel structure, the term parallelism usually refers to dependent clauses, phrases, and words.

> NOT PARALLEL: I'll tell you about Luther's home run, his double play, and how he stole two bases.
>
> ANALYSIS:
> Luther's home run, (**noun phrase**)
> I'll tell you about his double play, (**noun phrase**)
> and how he stole two bases. (**noun clause**)
>
> PARALLEL: I'll tell you about Luther's home run, his double play, and his two stolen bases.
>
> NOT PARALLEL: After adjusting his headband, digging his sandals into the dirt, and he took a dozen practice swings, Luther was ready for the first pitch.

ANALYSIS:

After adjusting his headband, (**phrase**)
digging his sandals into the dirt, (**phrase**)
and he took a dozen practice swings, . . .
(**clause**)

PARALLEL: After adjusting his headband, digging in his sandals, and taking a dozen
practice swings, Luther was ready for the
first pitch.

When using correlative conjunctions (**either** . . .
or, neither . . . **nor, not** . . . **but, not only** . . . **but
also, both** . . . **and**), be sure that each correlative is
followed by the same grammatical structure.

NOT PARALLEL: Luther was **not only** tired
but also he was distracted.

ANALYSIS: The adjective **tired** follows **not
only**, while the clause **he was distracted**
follows **but also**. The most succinct correction will have both correlatives followed by
adjectives.

PARALLEL: Luther was **not only** tired **but
also** distracted.

NOT PARALLEL: I **neither** have the time **nor**
the ability to dig ants out of Osgood's glove.

ANALYSIS: The verb **have** follows **I**, while the
noun **ability** follows **nor**.

PARALLEL: I have **neither** the time **nor** the
ability to dig ants out of Osgood's glove.

Here are two parallel sentences worth admiring:

> Whenever I find myself growing grim about the mouth;
> whenever it is a damp, drizzly November in my soul;
> whenever I find myself involuntarily pausing before cof-
> fin warehouses, and bringing up the rear of every funer-
> al I meet; and especially whenever my hypos [morbid
> depressions] get such an upper hand of me, that it
> requires strong moral principle to prevent me from step-
> ping into the street and methodically knocking people's
> hats off – then, I account it high time to get to sea as
> soon as I can.
>
> Herman Melville

> The yellow fog that rubs its muzzle on the window-panes
> Licked its tongue into the corners of the evening,
> Lingered upon pools that stand in drains,
> Let fall upon its back the soot that falls from chimneys,
> Slipped by the terrace, made a sudden leap,
> And seeing that it was a soft October night,
> Curled once about the house, and fell asleep.
>
> T. S. Eliot

PRACTICE SENTENCES

Parallelism

DIRECTIONS: On a separate piece of paper, write out
the following sentences correctly. If the sentence contains no errors, simply write a C.

1. Sally runs fast, thinks quickly, and has a great
   attitude.
2. Casey stepped up to the plate, stared at the pitcher, and then took his stance.
3. My brother enjoys mountain biking, and he also
   hang-glides.

4. Exhausted from her journey and famished from lack of food, Jane collapsed.

5. The job candidate seemed intelligent, articulate, and had solid references.

6. Elroy promised to meet us at the concert and that he would give us a ride home afterward.

7. I have and will continue to be a strong advocate for the rights of children.

8. Prunella's home-grown tomatoes were juicier than Martin.

9. John woke up, got out of bed, and dragged a comb across his head.

10. As a college freshman, he studied not only Spanish, but he also took Latin and Swahili.

11. After slamming her adversary into the boards and she retrieved the puck from the corner, Gertrude darted around the net and slipped the puck past the sprawling goalie.

12. Students sat expectantly in their seats, waiting for the Head of School to speak and they hoped he would announce a Mountain Day.

13. Ronald could recall neither the author's name nor could he recall the book's title.

14. Florence's goals were to attend Harvard, major in comparative religions, and she wanted to study with Robert Coles.

15. The pianist glared at the keyboard, raised his hands above the keys, and the Liszt Fantasy began in a furious barrage of notes.

SOURCES OF WORDINESS

Lack of subordination creates choppy, wordy writing; nonparallel sentences usually contain extra words; and the passive voice adds at least two words (**The ball was hit by Luther** compared to **Luther hit the ball**). Shaping sentences means not only presenting the action directly and clearly, but also excluding meaningless or vague language.

VERBAL FALSE LIMBS

George Orwell invented this term to describe our habit of turning strong verbs into nouns or adjectives and then substituting weak verbs.

Wordy	*Tight*
that gives the warning	that warns
to be envious of	to envy
to have an effect upon	to affect
to be suspicious of	to suspect
that is the cause of	that causes
to put into preservation	to preserve

Always seek the strong verb!

GENERAL VERBS

Beware of using too many all-purpose verbs like these: **to be** (am, was, were), **to have**, **to show**, **to make**, **to use**, **to give**, **to go**. Look for the verb that describes a specific action.

WEAK VERB: Marybelle **is** a .300 batter.

STRONG VERB: Marybelle **bats** .300.

FAT PHRASES

Avoid wordy phrases like these:	Instead, use these:
all too often	often
due to the fact that	since, because
in order to	to
as to whether	whether
by means of	by
for the purpose of	for
he is a man who	he
this story is a strange one	this strange story

EMPTY NOUNS

Nouns like these stand for something but have little meaning of their own: **element**, **quality**, **nature** (the nature of), **case**, **aspect**, **fact** (the fact that), **relationship**, **thing**, **one** (one of).

> WORDY: At first the **relationship** between Macbeth and Banquo is one of **friendship**.

> TIGHT: At first Macbeth and Banquo are friends.
> or
> Friends at first, Macbeth and Banquo . . .

THERE IS

WORDY: **There is** a character named Macbeth who becomes king.
TIGHT: Macbeth becomes king.

TAUTOLOGY

(Saying the same thing twice)

Ex. –

free gift	female goddess
my own personal	local townspeople
final ultimatum	many various
last and final	many different
five in number	mentally insane
dissolve away	new departure
orally aloud	refer back
perfectly correct	true facts
emotionally worried	gather together
completely surrounded	continue on
foreign immigrants	blue in color
brainstorming ideas	inject in
large in size	meet together

WORDY CONSTRUCTIONS

WORDY: **In this essay about** *Macbeth*, **I will show that** the three witches are in control of the action in the play.

TIGHT: The three witches control the action in Shakespeare's *Macbeth*.

VAGUE ADJECTIVES AND ADVERBS

Instead of using vague adjectives and adverbs **show** exactly (with strong nouns and verbs) what happened and reread the section in this book called "Good Ground" (pages 11-16).

nice	awesome	marvelous
good	excellent	fantastic
bad	very	pretty (adv.)
unbelievable	rather	great
horrible	amazing	
awful	almost	

PRACTICE SENTENCES

Wordy, Spelling, and Word Choice

DIRECTIONS: On a separate piece of paper, write out the following sentences correctly. If the sentence contains no errors, simply write a *C*.

1. The maple tree has recieved an attack by tent caterpillars.
2. John was hoping to be given warning of the forest fire.
3. Siena is envious of Jeannette's unlimitted allowance.
4. No one referred to Jerry, who was actually the cause of the error at third base.
5. Mary always earns a one hundred percent on the weekly etymology quizes.
6. While singeing her eyebrows, Earlene all too often burns herself.
7. Due to the fact that canoeing can be dangerous, we all wear lifejackets.
8. While shoeing the horses, he is a man who is very careful.
9. Harry was not decieved by means of the pitcher's curve ball.
10. For the purpose of finding the Jones'es house, Tom asked his mother where they lived.
11. The concert was an odd one because in about half of the songs, the band sang without playing on their instruments.
12. In order to understand the affects of the drought, we will have to visit the farms effected.
13. Since she possessed the quality of flexibility, Mary adopted easily to living abroad.

14. It is not the nature of George's eyes to be easily aggravated.
15. The fact that we have arrived all ready, suggests that we are anxious for the game to begin.
16. The relationship between the two of us is one of an improving quality.
17. Joyce received a large amount of free gifts for her birthday.
18. Bring me to your own personal leader.
19. We continued on a mile further.
20. I'd be mentally insane to eat the huge desert!
21. Partner, why don't we corroborate and brainstorm some ideas?
22. Everyone complemented me on finally buying my own personal blazer.
23. Ray seems continuously emotionally worried.
24. In this essay about the causes of World War I, I will sight a large amount of cause.
25. Although the book is large in size, we will cover less chapters then usual.
26. The female goddess looses her power on poor Odysseus.
27. The hole world would of benefitted in many, various ways.
28. Should I infer from your stern voice that this is the final ultimatum?
29. Its a case of too many foreign immigrants for the city to absorb in one month.
30. The dog laying in the middle of the floor is large in size.
31. Mr. Pepper, please lie down your red pen and explain my mistake to me.
32. Since Joan was emotionally worried, she laid down for a rest.
33. I had lain down most of the afternoon for the purpose of resting my bad leg.

34. We preceded to ask the local townspeople for advice.
35. Bob refered back to the fact that we planned to revenge last year's three-to-two loss to Hill Top Academy.
36. The principal reason for the countrys new departure into plastics is the fact that they need a new line of products.
37. The school gathers together quit often.
38. Just stand their stationery; I think were completely surrounded.
39. We meet together more then twice a week.
40. What color are pucks? I think their black in color.
41. I to want to learn the true facts.
42. When good judges listen to orally aloud testimony, they remain uninterested.
43. The coach seemed disinterested in the nature of why I came late to practice.
44. We are now aware of the tortuous conditions in Turkey.
45. All too often we don't know whether the whether will change or not.
46. This is the which whom I believe carried the large in size broomstick.
47. Who do you think will be elected?
48. I'm not sure whom to invite.
49. Your never sure who you think will make the best captain.
50. Who's car belong to who?

SENTENCE VARIETY

Avoid the subject-verb-object (SVO) rut by using introductory elements (prepositional phrases, participial phrases, adverb clauses), by placing appositive and absolute phrases after the verb, and by varying the length and structure of sentences.

Two alternatives to the SVO rut:

Periodic Sentence: (the main idea comes last)

> Ex. – On the seventh pitch Luther, who had not yet lifted his bat from his shoulder, connected.

Inversion: (subject follows verb)

> Ex. – Somewhere in the six-foot-high goldenrod and Queen Anne's lace that littered center field lurked Luther's ancient enemy – Elven Wood.

While amateur writers tend to place most of their ideas before the subject, professionals often withhold ideas until after the verb. Here is an amateurish sentence that states its main ideas first and then offers a dull, anticlimactic verb:

> After hiking up Black Rock, visiting Elven Wood in his tree house, and getting back home after dark, Osgood was tired.

In the following two excerpts from the end of *The Great Gatsby*, F. Scott Fitzgerald extends his sentences beyond their expected conclusions. In the first sentence, Fitzgerald uses an adverb clause (until . . .) followed by a delayed appositive phrase (a fresh . . .).

SVO

And as the moon rose higher the inessential houses began to melt away until gradually I became aware of the old island here that flowered once for Dutch sailors' eyes – a fresh, green breast of the new world.

Fitzgerald has gracefully and usefully added twenty-five words after **away**, the sentence's likely conclusion.

In this second sentence, the novel's last, Fitzgerald gives us a four-word main clause, then adds two more phrases.

So we beat on, boats against the current, borne back ceaselessly into the past.

By withholding the two phrases, Fitzgerald creates a powerful sentence and avoids one as undistinguished as this:

So with our boats against the current but still being borne back ceaselessly into the past, we beat on.

WRITING EXERCISE

Write ten pairs of sentences, the first of each pair being an SVO construction and the second an interesting alternative, such as a periodic sentence or an inverted sentence. You may use the examples above as models for some of your sentences.

BEING CORRECT

I have never thought of myself as a good writer. Anyone who wants reassurance of that should read one of my first drafts. But I'm one of the world's great rewriters.

I find that three or four readings are required to comb out the cliches, line up pronouns with antecedents, and insure agreement in number between subjects and verbs. It is, however, this hard work that produces style. You write the first draft really to see how it's going to come out.

My connectives, my clauses, my subsidiary phrases don't come naturally to me and I'm very prone to repetition of words; so I never even write an important letter in one draft. I can never recall anything of mine that's ever been printed in less than three drafts.

James A. Michener

Ironically, the **last** things you do with your writing (correct spelling errors, agreement problems, sentence errors, vague references of pronouns, etc.) are the **first** things your reader notices. Because a teacher encounters many technical errors in student papers, it is easy to see that he or she may unconsciously equate good writing with correct writing. On the other hand, if your writing is correct, your teacher-reader, undistracted by glaring errors, will be better able to appreciate your paper's content and style.

As you edit your papers, don't forget James Michener and all the other writers who find it difficult to be correct. "This hard work" of correcting errors, Mr. Michener reminds us, "produces style."

WRITING WORDS CORRECTLY

LEG

LEGIBILITY

If your readers cannot read your writing, or if they have to reread it to decipher your manuscript, print! Or type. Or, best of all, use a word processor.

SP

FIVE SPELLING RULES

1. Adding suffixes to words ending in a final consonant.

    a. For one-syllable words that end in a single consonant preceded by a single vowel, double the final consonant for suffixes beginning with a vowel.

    Ex. - hop – hopping   sin – sinful
          trip – tripped   BUT   man – manly

    b. For words of more than one syllable, double the final consonant if the accent is on the last syllable.

    Ex. - om**it** – omitted   **lim**it – limited
          re**fer** – referring   BUT   **num**ber – numbered

2. Adding a suffix to words ending in a silent **e**.

    a. If the suffix begins with a vowel, drop the **e**.

    Ex. - hope – hoping
          scrape – scraped

    b. If the suffix begins with a consonant, keep the **e**.

    Ex. - hope – hopeful
          pride – prideful

EXCEPTIONS:

1) Tr**ul**y, Mr. D**ul**y, your ni**n**th arg**um**ent is who**ll**y a**wf**ul.
   That is an acknowled**gm**ent of your jud**gm**ent.

2) To retain the soft sound in words (such as the **g** in change or the **c** in notice) keep the **e** before suffixes beginning with **a, o** and **u** (chang**ea**ble, outrag**eo**us, notic**ea**ble, and servic**ea**ble.

3) **Dyeing** and **singeing** keep the **e** so as not to be confused with **dying** and **singing**.

4) **Canoeing, hoeing, tiptoeing**, and **shoeing** keep the **e** to avoid the **oi** sound of c**oi**n and j**oi**n.

3. Adding suffixes to words ending in **y**.

The letter **y** following a consonant changes to **i** except before an **i** suffix.

Ex. - cry – cried   cry – crying
    satisfy – satisfied   **BUT**   satisfy – satisfying

Note that the **y**'s in the following words follow vowels and thus do not change: **prayed, valleys, chimneys, pulleys, enjoyment**.

EXCEPTIONS: **Laid, paid, said, slain, daily**

4. IE, EI or EIGH.

Use **i** before **e** (**chief, brief, piece, niece, field,** etc.) except after "c" (**receive, deceive, receipt,** etc.) or when sounding like **a** (**vein, veil, reins, reign, freight**) as in **neighbor** or **weigh**.

EXCEPTIONS: Neither leisured foreigner seized the weird heights.
Forfeit counterfeit heifer protein.

An ancient species of man had a conscience like a glacier. (Note that we keep the i before the e to retain the sh sound of ci.)

POS   5. Forming possessives.

Follow this procedure for forming possessives:

a. Write out the desired number of your noun – singular or plural.

   Ex. – Mountains (plural)

b. Add the sign of the possessive (apostrophe and **s**);

   Ex. – Mountains**'s**

c. If an **s** immediately precedes your apostrophe, drop the **s** following your apostrophe.

   Ex. – Mountains' (the plural possessive of mountain)

Ex. – SINGULAR POSSESSIVE | PLURAL POSSESSIVE
dog's | (dogs's) dogs'
(Morris's) Morris' | (Morrises's) Morrises'
person's | people's

EXCEPTIONS:
a. In forming the singular possessive of a noun ending in s, you have the option of either retaining or dropping the s following the apostrophe.

   Ex. – Morris's car OR Morris' car.

b. Do not use an apostrophe with the personal pronoun in the possessive case: his, hers, its, ours, yours, theirs, and the relative pronoun whose.

CAPITALIZATION CAP

Capitalize the following:

1. Proper names: France, New York, Shakespeare

2. Proper adjectives: French, New Yorker, Shakespearean

3. Organizations: Chess Club, Student Life Committee

4. Religions, races, cultures: Protestant, Negro, Japanese

5. Places: Santa Barbara, Chester County, Iowa, Italy, Asia

6. Important events: Battle of the Bulge, Middle Ages, Cold War, Earth Day, Junior Prom

7. Particular places or things such as ships, planes, and documents: the Queen Elizabeth, the Bill of Rights, the Washington Monument, Mount Fuji, Fifth Avenue

8. The first words and all other words in titles of books, short stories, poems, articles, etc., except articles, conjunctions, and prepositions: *The Heart of the Matter*.

9. Titles and family relationships when they are not preceded by a possessive pronoun:

   Ex. – This is Dr. William Rush, our family doctor.

   Ex. – My mother is waiting for Dad and Uncle Al.

Do not capitalize common nouns, such as **town**, **city**, **road**, **street**, **freshman**, **college**, **bank**.

> Ex. – The sophomores decorated for the Junior Prom.

We capitalize "Junior" because it is part of the name of an important event.

10. Capitalize days and months, but not seasons.

> Ex. – By the first Sunday in October, fall had arrived.

11. Capitalize directions when they represent a geographical area, but not when they indicate a direction.

> Ex. – If you head north, you will reach the Mason and Dixon's line, which divides North and South.

CONFUSING PAIRS OF WORDS

ACCEPT and **EXCEPT**

Since everyone **except** Luther **accepted** the invitation, Luther **excepted** (excluded) himself.

ADOPT and **ADAPT**

Monica **adapted** to the difficult situation.

Marybelle **adopted** a stray dog.

AFFECT and **EFFECT**

Do you know how the **effects** (noun, "results") of the program **affected** (verb, "influenced") farmers?

AGGRAVATE and IRRITATE

I am **irritated** (annoyed) not only because these new contact lenses **irritate** (inflame or make sore) my eyes, but also because this windy weather **aggravates** (makes worse) the condition.

ALL RIGHT and ALREADY

All right, you may play, but the game has **already** begun.

AMONG and BETWEEN

Just **between** the two of us, I think that we are **among** several serious students.

AMOUNT and NUMBER

A **number** of students complained about the small **amount** of free time and the large **amount** of homework.

BRING and TAKE

Bring (to) me another watermelon and **take** (from me) this rind.

COMPLIMENT and COMPLEMENT

Osgood **complimented** Marybelle on how well her red shorts **complemented** her blue sneakers.

CONSCIOUS, CONSCIENTIOUS, CONSCIENCE

Marybelle's **conscience** always bothered her if she did not **consciously** try to be a **conscientious** team player.

CONTINUAL and CONTINUOUS

Martha's **continual** (repeated often) interruptions disturbed what I had hoped would be my **continuous** (unbroken) train of thought.

CORROBORATE and COLLABORATE

The writer **corroborated** (confirmed) the story that he and a fellow writer had **collaborated** (worked together) on the novel.

DESERT and DESSERT

Luther says he'd rather cross a **desert** than **desert** a dinner table before **dessert**.

FARTHER and FURTHER

The **farther** (a measurable distance) we had to run, the **further** (additionally) annoyed we became.

FEWER and LESS

If we had **less** time in class, we would cover **fewer** chapters of the text.

GOOD and WELL

No one is surprised when a **good** (adjective) team plays **well** (adverb).

HAVE and OF

You must **have** (not **of**) heard of Elven Wood, the elusive center fielder.

HOLE and WHOLE

The **whole** family of foxes ran down the **hole** in the hillside.

ILLUSION, ALLUSION, ALLUDE, ELUDE

Luther **alluded** (referred) to Plato's philosophy when he said that softball is an **illusion** – no more a reality than elves and magic bats. Not even Osgood, who was busy **eluding** a wasp, recognized Luther's **allusion** to Plato.

IMPLY and INFER

Are you **implying** that we should leave tonight?

I **infer** from your comments that you think we should leave tonight.

INCREDIBLE and INCREDULOUS

Marybelle looked **incredulous** (unbelieving) when Elven Wood wagged his **incredible** (unbelievable) ears.

ITS and IT'S

It's (It is) a pleasure to hear **its** (possessive) motor running well.

LIE, LYING, LAY, LAIN (to recline) and LAY, LAYING, LAID, LAID (to place)

PRESENT: **Lay** down the book and **lie** down to rest.

PAST: Yesterday she **laid** down the book and **lay** down to rest.

89

PAST PERFECT: After she had **laid** (placed) down the book and had **lain** (reclined) down to rest, a softball came flying through her window.

Note that the present tense of **lay** and the past tense of **lie** are both **lay**.

LOOSE and LOSE

Don't **lose** that **loose** hat.

NO ONE, NO, KNOW

No, we don't **know** for certain that **no one** can go.

PROCEED and PRECEDE

When they **proceeded** (went on) to the church, Monica's car **preceded** (came before) Osgood's.

PRINCIPLE and PRINCIPAL

When the **principal** (head) stated his **principal** (main) concerns, we realized that he was a man of **principle** (rule of conduct).

QUIET and QUITE

It's **quite** a **quiet** day.

REVENGE and AVENGE

To **avenge** (verb) his ancient people, Elven Wood sought **revenge** (noun) upon Luther.

STATIONARY and STATIONERY

Monica's lime green **stationery** (writing paper) has been **stationary** (motionless) since she received it from Aunt Gigi.

THEN and THAN

Then (at that time) Osgood said that an olive oiled glove was more honest **than** (introduces an unequal comparison) a magic bat.

THERE, THEIR, THEY'RE

They're (they are) **there** (a place) with **their** (possessive) little brothers.

TO, TOO, TWO

Two dirty dogs wanted **to** play **too** (also).

TORTUOUS and TORTUROUS

Climbing the **tortuous** (winding, twisting) path was **torturous** (involving torture).

UNINTERESTED and DISINTERESTED

A **disinterested** (unprejudiced) spectator said the ball was fair.

The **uninterested** (not interested) student daydreamed during the lecture on Charles Dickens.

WE'RE, WERE, WHERE

We're (we are) in a class **where** two students spell **were** with an *h*.

WHETHER and WEATHER

Whether or not we go depends upon the **weather**.

WHICH and **WITCH**

Ms. Goodie, that old **witch**, says, "Don't forget the first *h* in **which**."

WHO and **WHOM** (see Page 107)

Bill Allan, **who** (nominative case) lives next door, sold his car to a boy **whom** (objective case) we know.

WHO'S and **WHOSE**

Who's (who is) the person **whose** (possessive) sister called?

YOUR and **YOU'RE**

Your (possessive) mother remembered **you're** (you are) coming to the party.

PRACTICE SENTENCES

The practice sentences for **Spelling** and **Word Choice** are combined with **Wordy** on page 76.

Capitalization and a Review of Punctuation

DIRECTIONS: Correct the error or errors in the following sentences, and in the space at the left write the appropriate number(s) of the punctuation rule(s) that was(were) broken. Place a *C* before sentences that are correct.

_____ 1. On july 10 1997 dad drove all the way to the national gallery in washington d.c. where he met aunt sally they were looking for their favorite thomas cole painting entitled kindred spirits.

_____ 2. If you spend a semester in china your chinese will undoubtedly improve

_____ 3. Japanese taiwanese indonesian indian vietnamese and korean kids all belong to the school's asia society the religion club has buddhists catholics hindus jews moslims and protestants

_____ 4. During the renaissance the english language gained hundreds of latin words most of which were used by william shakespeare

_____ 5. In chapter XVII entitled The grangerfords take me in of the adventures of huckleberry finn mark twain includes a poem ode to stephen dowling bots, dec'd.

_____ 6. my friend officer coney lives on a little street called petunia way a block from the first national bank in newark delaware a few miles south of wilmington.

_____ 7. Now that fall has come to the east tony can think of only one thing footballs spiraling through clear blue skies against yellow and red backdrops.

_____ 8. Drive south ten miles on the old post road hop on the mass. pike get off at the lee exit and follow the signs to stockbridge the former home of norman rockwell and now a popular tourist trap.

_____ 9. Are you sure mother asked Is the roast cooked yet

_____ 10. No mary I don't know who produced the movie Fargo.

WRITING SENTENCES CORRECTLY

SE   SENTENCE ERRORS

Avoid all forms of sentence errors: sentence fragments, comma splices, and run-on sentences.

FRAG   1.   A sentence **fragment** is a word, phrase, or clause
punctuated as a sentence.

ERROR: Do you know why Marybelle climbed
Black Rock? **Because she was looking for
elves**.

Note that the fragment, an adverbial clause,
sounds like a complete sentence because the
missing main clause is understood.

CORRECTION: Marybelle went up to Black Rock
because she was looking for elves.

or

Do you know that Marybelle went up to Black
Rock to look for elves?

In personal papers that imitate everyday speech
patterns, the fragment is necessary and appropriate, but it is **inappropriate in academic
papers**.

CS   2.   The **comma splice** uses a comma to join two independent clauses.

ERROR: We were tired from climbing, the trip had
taken only thirty minutes.

CORRECTION: We were tired from climbing; the
trip had taken only thirty minutes.

or (better)
We were tired from climbing, although the trip had taken only thirty minutes.

3. *Conjunctive adverbs*. When we use adverbs like **then**, **however**, **nevertheless**, **moreover**, **also**, and **therefore** to join main clauses, we must precede the adverb with a semicolon.

ERROR: The trip had taken only thirty minutes, nevertheless, we were tired from climbing.

CORRECTION: The trip had taken only thirty minutes; nevertheless, we were tired from climbing.

4. The **run-on** sentence joins two main clauses without using either a semicolon or a comma with a coordinating conjunction (FANBOY – for, and, nor, but, or, yet).

RO

ERROR: We looked up a peregrine falcon flew from its nest high on Black Rock.

CORRECTION: We looked up, and a peregrine falcon flew from its nest high on Black Rock.
or (better)
As we looked up, a peregrine falcon flew from its nest high on Black Rock.

Note that compound sentences usually can be subordinated.

PRACTICE SENTENCES

Sentence Errors: FRAGMENTS, COMMA SPLICES, AND RUN-ONS

DIRECTIONS: On a separate piece of paper, write out the following sentences correctly. If the sentence contains no errors, simply write a *C*.

1. Mary playing golf.
2. Mary is playing golf.
3. Mary plays golf.
4. Since Mary plays golf.
5. All one thousand of us enjoyed the concert. Because Phish is the best band since the Dead.
6. Then the class was over.
7. When the class was over.
8. We began late, you had probably already started home.
9. He felt fine he was just upset for a moment.
10. Thirty-two people went to the game, it was excellent.
11. Mr. Merrill is frowning, you had better stop humming.
12. Mr. Merrill is frowning; you had better stop humming.
13. Since Mr. Merrill is frowning you had better stop humming.
14. The bike was in demand. Because it was cool.
15. I caught three fish, we had them for dinner.
16. I work in a deli I enjoy eating food.
17. The big, black dog named Zack.
18. I like to swim; thus I want a pool.
19. The night was long we stayed up for seven hours.
20. I am cold. Because I am wet.

21. Clear the track here comes the first runner.
22. Glenny Brook is still running because we've had rain all summer.
23. The chair was comfortable I sat in it.
24. The new teacher with a beautiful wife.
25. I looked at my ties; I picked one from the rack.
26. I looked at my ties, I picked one from the rack.
27. Because I looked at my ties. I picked one from the rack.
28. The dog was fat he took up too much room in the car.
29. The dog was fat, he took up too much room in the car.
30. Lying on top of the mountain without a jacket in below zero weather.
31. Because I fed my dog Purina dog chow.
32. After dinner we all had ice cream; I had vanilla.
33. After dinner we all had ice cream, I had vanilla.
34. After dinner we all had ice cream. I had vanilla.
35. Everybody wanted tickets. Because they love Phish.
36. He is reading *Walden*, he has no idea what it means.
37. I am too young. My father does not want me to drive.
38. You went to Japan last summer because you won first prize.
39. Stop lying I will not be your friend.
40. He has a car and he drives too fast.

1. A noun coming between the subject and its verb can be confusing.

   ERROR: The **trails** up the mountain **begins** in the same place.

   CORRECTION: The **trails** up the mountain **begin** in the same place.

2. Again, remember that these indefinite pronouns are **singular**:

anybody	everybody	no one
anyone	every one	one
each	everyone	somebody
either	neither	someone

   Ex. – **Everyone climbs** (not climb) up to Black Rock.
   Ex. – **Each** of the three thousand men **carries** (not carry) **his** (not their) own equipment.

3. These words are **plural: both, few, many, several**.

   Ex. – **Few** of Luther's friends **understand** him.

4. These words are **singular** or **plural**, depending on the meaning of the sentence: **all, any, most, none, some**.

   Ex. – **All** the preparation **seems** complete.
   Ex. – **All** of the players **like** Marybelle.

5. Compound subjects take plural verbs.

   Ex. – **Osgood and Luther** rarely **argue**.

6. Beware of long, possibly confusing phrases that   **AGR**
come between a subject and its verb.

Ex. – **Osgood** (subject) as well as most of his
friends **takes** (verb) softball seriously.

Ex. – **Part** (subject) of the difficulty with identifying spring warblers **is** (verb) simply seeing
these small birds.

7. When a subject is joined by **or** or **nor**, the verb
agrees with the nearer subject.

Ex. – Neither the players nor the **coach likes**
Luther's lemonade.
Ex. – Neither the coach nor the **players like**
Luther's lemonade.

8. Collective nouns may be singular (the group as a
whole) or plural (the group as separate individuals).

Ex. – The **team were** arguing about Luther's bat.
Ex. – The team **was convinced** that Luther had
polluted the lemonade.

AGREEMENT OF PRONOUN   **AGR**
AND ANTECEDENT

Pronouns must agree in number and gender with
their antecedents, the nouns to which pronouns refer.

Ex. – **Luther** said **he** did not use Ironwood, his
bat, to stir the lemonade.

1. Again, remember the singular indefinite pronouns

listed previously in Agreement of Subject and Verb.

> Ex. – If **anybody** drinks that lemonade, watch **him** carefully.
> Ex. – **Each** took **his** turn.

2. Use a singular pronoun to refer to singular nouns joined by **or** or **nor**.

> Ex. – Neither Monica **nor** Marybelle has given **her** opinion of Luther's concoction.

3. When **neither** . . . **nor** or **either** . . . **or** join the subjects of a sentence, the verb agrees with the nearer subject.

> Ex. – Either Monica or her **parents have** brought donuts to the game.
> Ex. – Either the parents or **Monica has** brought donuts to the game.

4. Use a plural pronoun to refer to two or more singular nouns joined by **and**.

> Ex. – Monica **and** Marybelle have not given **their** opinions.

PRACTICE SENTENCES

Agreement: SUBJECT-VERB AGREEMENT and PRONOUN-ANTECEDENT AGREEMENT

DIRECTIONS: On a separate piece of paper, write out the following sentences correctly. If the sentence contains no errors, simply write a *C*.

1. The sun is warm and bright, and around him is acres of grain.
2. The kid with all the friend always seem happy.
3. Is the lady and the tramp friends?
4. A group of teachers who are not afraid to change the rules break into the gym.
5. Not only Charlie but also Billy are running the race this summer.
6. The students' problem are their many distractions.
7. The desire of students are good grades.
8. Ethics are his least favorite class.
9. There is many styles of music on local radio shows.
10. Neither of them were eager for the evening to end.
11. Are politics always corrupt?
12. Neither my brother nor my sister are here.
13. There remain only a few rattlesnakes on Black Rock.
14. She has an obsession for those type of people.
15. He desires those kind of flowers.
16. My best friend and sister have arrived. [sister is the best friend]
17. A flock of sea gulls dives through the garbage.
18. They think Eli have no right to do that.
19. Both Sally and I am hoping to be in the play.
20. Skiing and golfing is my favorite sports.
21. Not all of the course are dry yet.
22. The reason for the storms as well as the earthquake are hard to understand.
23. Neither Bill nor his parents is home.
24. Both my mother and father is coming to visit.
25. The class were confused about the assignment.
26. Everybody should return their uniforms.
27. Neither of them were ready to graduate in April.
28. Either Melissa or one of her parents is at the store.
29. The team of scientists are not studying butterflies this semester.

30. A swarm of bees are heading for his head.
31. If she was an experienced climber, she would not have fallen to her death.
32. The crowd of shoppers are running out of the burning mall.
33. A pack of wolves are starting for the wounded leopard.
34. He dances to those kind of songs.
35. Elaine want to travel to Morocco.
36. A man sell pipes at the crossroads.
37. Eating and drinking is Nora's greatest pleasure.
38. Both Lucy and her aunt Lida is flying to Kiribis for fly-fishing.
39. Neither Chaucer nor Shakespeare are still alive.
40. The class were debating the theme of *A Farewell to Arms*.
41. The doctor's concern are her heart patients.
42. My cousin are at the triathlon in Canada.
43. Molly along with her roommate run with the president on Thursdays.
44. None of us is going to the game.
45. Everybody must remain in their seats.
46. Neither the Orphum nor the Wang are holding concerts tonight.
47. Arguing and winning are what makes her a lawyer of distinction.
48. Korean and Japanese is Uki's first languages.
49. Slang are a big part of English.
50. Hong Kong and China is reuniting in the summer of 1997.

The antecedents of pronouns must be nouns – not phrases, not clauses, and not whole sentences. Here are some common problems with pronoun reference.

1. **Ambiguous Reference**: a pronoun with more than one possible antecedent.

   ERROR: Osgood told Luther that he was sick.

   CORRECTION: Osgood told Luther, "You are sick."
   or
   Osgood told Luther, "I am sick."

2. **Broad Reference of Pronoun**: a pronoun that refers to a whole phrase or a sentence. This error usually involves **which** or **this**.

   ERROR: Luther was tired, **which** accounted for his pale face.

   CORRECTION: Luther looked pale because he was tired.

   ERROR: Marybelle looked pale also. **This** made Monica wonder about the lemonade.

   CORRECTION: Marybelle's pale face made Monica wonder about the lemonade.
   or
   When Marybelle began to look pale, Monica wondered about the lemonade.

3. **Vague Reference**: a pronoun that has an implied but unstated antecedent.

   ERROR: **They** say it will rain.

CORRECTION: The weatherman predicted rain.

ERROR: The author, protesting that his novels were not romantic, said that contemporary writers rejected **it**.

CORRECTION: The author, protesting that his novels were not romantic, said that contemporary writers rejected romanticism.

ERROR: Jogging through the woods is not as harmful to your back as jogging on paved roads, because **they** are not jarring.

CORRECTION: Jogging through the woods on dirt trails is not as harmful to your back as jogging on paved roads.

ERROR: **It** says Frederic Henry rowed across Lake Geneva.

CORRECTION: Frederic Henry rowed across Lake Geneva.

ERROR: In Hemingway's *A Farewell to Arms,* **he** sets the novel in Italy and Switzerland.

CORRECTION: Hemingway sets *A Farewell to Arms* in Italy and Switzerland.

Note that the **he** in the error above cannot refer clearly to **Hemingway's**, which is acting as an adjective.

SOME HUMOROUS PROBLEMS
WITH REFERENCE OF PRONOUN

Try to identify the kind of reference error in each of these examples taken from Richard Lederer's *Anguished English* (Wyrick & Co.).

— Guilt, vengeance, and bitterness can be emotionally destructive to you and your children. You must get rid of them.
— Anti-nuclear protestors released live cockroaches inside the White House Friday, and these were arrested when they left and blocked a security gate.
— Great care must always be exercised in tethering horses to trees as they are apt to bark.
— A fortune cookie message: You have many personal talents that are attractive to others, so be sure to use them.
— Two cycles belonging to girls that had been left leaning against lamp-posts were badly damaged.
— My mother wants to have the dog's tail operated on again, and if it doesn't heal this time, she'll have to be put away.
— Jerry Remy then hit an RBI single off Haas's leg, which rolled into right field.
— About two years ago, a wart appeared on my left hand, which I wanted removed.
— On the floor above him lived a redheaded instructor in physical education, whose muscular calves he admired when they nodded to each other by the mailbox.
— Do not park your car at the taxi stand or it will be towed away.

CASE OF PRONOUNS

Use pronouns in the correct case.

1. Do not confuse nominative pronouns with objective pronouns. Use nominative pronouns – **I**, **you**, **he**, **she**, **it**, **we**, **you**, **they** – as subjects and as predicate nominatives.

> Ex. – **We** walked in the woods.
> Ex. – It was **we** who were in the woods.

Use objective pronouns – **me**, **you**, **him**, **her**, **it**, **us**, **you**, **them** – as objects.

> Ex. – Ask Osgood about Monica and **us**.
> Ex. – Luther told Monica and **me**.
> Ex. – The secret remains between you and **me**.

2. Use the possessive case before a gerund.

> Ex. – Elven Wood doesn't like **my** climbing up to Black Rock.

3. Use appositives in the case of the noun to which they refer.

> Ex. – Elven invited all of us – Marybelle, Osgood, Luther, Monica, and **me** – to his tree house.
> Ex. – The players – Elven, Luther, Marybelle, Osgood, Monica, and **I** – had a party in Elven's tree house.

4. Use reflexive pronouns (myself, yourself, himself, herself, itself, oneself, ourselves, yourselves, themselves) to describe action that the subject directs to himself.

Ex. – Elven hurt himself on the ladder.
Ex. – Marybelle asked herself why Elven lived in a tree.

— and to intensify an idea.

Ex. – Elven **himself** loved life in the trees.

Do not use reflexives as subjects.

ERROR: Monica and **myself** loved Elven's tree house.

CORRECTION: Monica and **I** loved Elven's tree house.

Do not use a reflexive pronoun as an object if the subject is different from the object.

ERROR: Elven asked Monica and **myself** to visit some of his forest friends.

CORRECTION: Elven asked Monica and **me** to visit some of his forest friends.

5. **Who** and **whom**

As relative pronouns, **who** is nominative and **whom** objective.

Ex. – Elven introduced us to Legolas, **who** bowed majestically. Legolas is a brave elf **whom** J.R.R. Tolkien created in *The Lord of the Rings*.

Here is a way to tell whether **who** or **whom** is correct:

When **who** or **whom** is followed by the subject of

the dependent clause, **whom** is the correct pronoun. When, however, **who** or **whom** is followed by a verb, **who** is the subject of that verb.

EXCEPTIONS: This rule works unless a parenthetical clause follows the **who** or **whom** or the verb is a form of **to be**.

Ex. – Legolas is the same elf who, **you recall**, lived in Lorien.

Don't let the **you recall** mislead you. It is not part of the sentence's structure. **Who** is the subject of lived and thus should remain **who**.

Ex. – I don't know who Legolas **is**.

MISPLACED MODIFIERS

MOD

Place your modifiers as close as possible to the words they modify.

ERROR: After **almost** resting an hour, the team began the seventh inning. (misplaced adverb)

CORRECT: After resting **almost** an hour, the team began the seventh inning.

ERROR: Luther wrote that he'd like to leave Camp Heart Stone **in a letter**. (misplaced phrase)

CORRECT: Luther wrote **in a letter** that he'd like to leave Camp Heart Stone.

or

In a letter, Luther wrote that he'd like to leave Camp Heart Stone.

ERROR: The man will have prosperity **who rises early**. (misplaced clause)

CORRECT: The man **who rises early** will have prosperity.

Avoid squinting modifiers, modifiers that refer to either the preceding or the following word.

ERROR: Luther agreed **on the next day** to let Osgood make the lemonade.

CORRECT: **On the next** day Luther agreed to let Osgood make the lemonade.

Do not split infinitives.

ERROR: Osgood tried to **correctly** make lemonade.

CORRECT: Osgood tried to make lemonade **correctly**.

DANGLING MODIFIERS

Dangling modifiers are usually verbals that have nothing to modify.

ERROR: **While stirring the lemonade**, a sea gull flew overhead.

CORRECTION: While stirring the lemonade, Osgood saw a sea gull fly overhead.
or
While Osgood stirred the lemonade, he saw a sea gull fly overhead.

ERROR: **Before making lemonade**, a proper stirrer must be found.

CORRECTION: Before making lemonade, one must find a proper stirrer.

or

Before making lemonade, find a proper stirrer.

NOTE: To identify a dangling modifier, ask yourself who **did** whatever the dangling verbal is doing (Who **stirred** the lemonade? Who **made** the lemonade?). If the modifier is dangling, there will be no doer of that action (no stirrer, no maker). Then you must **add the doer of action** (**Osgood**, **one**, or an implied **you**).

SOME HUMOROUS PROBLEMS WITH MODIFICATION

Here are some more bloopers from Richard Lederer's *Anguished English* (Wyrick & Co.).

— Please take time to look over the brochure that is enclosed with your family.

— Plunging 1,000 feet into the gorge, we saw Yosemite Falls.

— CALF BORN TO FARMER WITH TWO HEADS

— Two cars were reported stolen by the Groveton Police yesterday.

— As a baboon who grew up wild in the jungle, I realized that Wiki had special nutritional needs.

— In 1979, he bought majority control of the company's stock, along with his mother.

— Do not sit in chair without being fully assembled.

— She died in the home in which she was born at the age of 88.

— Amy Carter was among more than 100 Americans returning from a 10-day tour of the Soviet Union during the weekend.

— Farmhand Joe Mobbs hoists a cow injured while giving birth to its feet.

IS WHEN, IS WHERE, AND IS BECAUSE

Avoid awkward constructions that try to use adverbial clauses as predicate nominatives.

ERROR: An example of symbolism is when a big apple stands for New York City.

CORRECTION: An example of symbolism is a big apple standing for New York City.

ERROR: The reason is because elves live in the forest around Black Rock.

CORRECTION: The reason is that elves live in the forest around Black Rock.

PRACTICE SENTENCES

Pronoun Reference, Case, Misplaced Modifiers, and Dangling Modifiers

DIRECTIONS: On a separate piece of paper, write out the following sentences correctly. If the sentence contains no errors, simply write a *C*.

PRONOUN REFERENCE AND MODIFIER ERRORS

1. "'Tis given out that, sleeping in my orchard, a serpent stung me."
2. The bird disappeared into the woods that we had seen earlier in the front yard.
3. While jogging with a friend along the beach, a dead seal appeared in the surf like a big, smelly rock.
4. Ms. Finneran asked Jane to represent the class because she is responsible and articulate.
5. After reading the rest of the play, her theory of why Macbeth murdered Duncan changed.
6. Although Tom enjoyed coaching football as part of his internship at Fox Run School, he does not intend to become one.
7. Missing for years in the attic of the old library, Mr. Sullivan found the notes of the school's first faculty meeting.
8. It says Macbeth and Lady Macbeth are ruthless murderers.
9. Running too fast, a wall bruised Mary's forehead and sprained her toe.
10. Tired from mowing the grass for two hours, the glass of ice tea was a treat.
11. Larry came late to first period class every day, which annoyed his teachers.
12. Tim dropped his glove as the ball bounced towards him, so he has to pick it up.
13. The new leaves are a deep green and still hanging loosely from their stems. This is beautiful.
14. They say we don't have a chance against Berger Academy.
15. Avoid leaving your book bag in the classroom or it will be taken away.

16. Having chipped the ball from the sand trap into the cup, the crowd applauded the golf pro.
17. I want to go to the movie tonight, but I have a paper due tomorrow, which is a problem.
18. Harry told his parents that he was leaving college in an e-mail message.
19. To help make sure everyone plays in the game, players are put on the field in units, rather than one at a time.
20. My father is a doctor, which is a profession that does not interest me.
21. In Shanghai they have wonder dumplings for sale on the streets.
22. We had to carry heavy canoes plus all of our gear on the canoe portages, which was too much to do in one trip.
23. Wearing her pink dress, Bill saw Mary going to the prom.
24. He had a new pair of Reeboks on his feet which he had purchased at Bob's Shoes.
25. Ms. Toner told Martha that she was no longer spending the summer in town.
26. In Shakespeare's *Hamlet*, he has the action take place in Denmark.
27. I heard about the robbery on the evening news.
28. Saying we needed to pay attention to it, Mr. Hall gave his famous lecture on the history of love and marriage.
29. The man was playing with his cat when he became annoyed and scratched him.
30. Good teachers like Mr. Marvel know that since distractions impede student progress, they have to be minimized.
31. Terry, a nice hockey player, can do it all winter without losing his interest.

32. I began painting the house, dressing in old clothes and dirty sneakers.
33. This book belongs to Mary that is about how to cook in the wilderness.
34. The robin sat on the fence, which began singing before dawn.
35. Bill laughed and told Harry he was a great guy.

PRONOUN CASE REVIEW

1. These are the students from who you must get some help.
2. Samuel and myself decided that we had to go to town.
3. He will give us boys advice and understanding.
4. All the actors who I know would like to play Hamlet.
5. We didn't want him driving my car without asking.
6. There are several characters who are difficult to understand in *Hamlet*.
7. The boss invited every one in the department – Peter, Suzanne Joe, Grover, and I – to the fancy dinner.
8. She gave herself a pat on the back for getting in all of her work on time.
9. These are the men, I think, who know how to solve the computer problem.
10. It is she who orders the supplies.
11. I didn't know who had gone on the search.
12. Mary and Margaret are the ones whom went to the fire.
13. Mr. Wale finally told John and me how to break the puck out of our zone.

14. Just between you and myself, I don't love pasta.
15. Janey, to whom I confided all my summer secrets, has told them to everyone in the dorm.
16. No one told Dick and myself that the bus is leaving early.
17. Tony is taller than him.
18. It was me who allowed the boys to leave class early.
19. The referee who he insulted kicked the coach out of the game.
20. Larry is one of the boys whom I have asked to be in the play.
21. If Mr. Hamilton hadn't repainted the wood-and-canvas canoes over the winter, today us campers would be painting, not paddling.
22. Who did you ask?
23. I don't like them complaining constantly about the homework.
24. Mom never liked my hiking alone.
25. Helen and I told them to rush the job.
26. He is one of those people who hand in work early.
27. I wonder who I should take to the prom.
28. Clyde Mather, who never used to dress up, has started wearing his grandfather's bow ties and his father's old tweed jackets.
29. Tom told us kids to meet him in town at noon.
30. It is I who built the clay tennis court.
31. Do anyone know about you and I?
32. Everyone knows it was him.
33. Did anyone remember that it was us who came in late?
34. Is it Arnold or she that will edit the yearbook?
35. The dean assigned Meg and I to cover Wednesday study halls.

Make sure your comparisons are logical and complete.

ERROR: Osgood said that Legolas' ears are as big as elephants. (Illogically, this sentence compares ears to elephants.)

CORRECTION: Osgood said that Legolas' ears are as big as an **elephant's ears**.

ERROR: Legolas is one of the **bravest** elves. (There can only be one brav**est**.)

CORRECTION: Legolas is one of the **braver** elves.

ERROR: Legolas is taller than any elf.

CORRECTION: Legolas is taller than any **other** elf.

ERROR: Lady Galadriel, the queen of the elves, is **so** beautiful.

CORRECTION: Lady Galadriel, the queen of the elves, is **so** beautiful **that** I can not forget her.

ERROR: Elven Wood is **such** a loyal elf.

CORRECTION: Elven Wood is **such** a loyal elf **that** he often visits Lady Galadriel.

Be careful to use the correct pronoun case when using comparative forms of adjectives and adverbs.

ERROR: Missy is a better skier than **me**.

CORRECTION: Missy is a better skier than **I**. (than I am)

ERROR: They played better than **us**.

CORRECTION: They played better than **we**. (than we played)

SUBJUNCTIVE MOOD

Use the subjunctive mood to express conditions contrary to fact.

> Ex. – If I **were** (not **was**) Elven, I'd miss Lorien.
> Ex. – I insisted that each of you **be** (not **is**) treated fairly.

DOUBLE NEGATIVES

Use one (**not two**) negative word to convey a negative meaning.

ERROR: Osgood is not scarcely ever on time.

CORRECTION: Osgood is scarcely ever on time.

ERROR: Osgood cannot hardly hit the ball.

CORRECTION: Osgood can hardly hit the ball.

Note that **scarcely** and **hardly** convey negative meanings.

LIKE VERSUS AS, AS IF, AS THOUGH

Do not use **like** as a conjunction. Instead, use **as**, **as though**, or **as if**.

ERROR: Osgood looks **like** he is tired.

CORRECTION: Osgood looks **as if** he is tired.

ERROR: It looks **like** the dog is dead.

CORRECTION: It looks **as though** the dog is dead.

FACTUAL ERROR

X

Know your subject well, and support your arguments with correct information.

WRITE OUT

W/O

Do not use informal abbreviations such as **w/** for **with** and **&** for **and**.

Write out numbers that are one or two words.

Ex. – Our library contains seven thousand volumes.

Always write out a number that begins a sentence.

Ex. – Two hundred and five children went to school today.

PRACTICE SENTENCES

Is When, Faulty Comparison, Mood, Double Negative, Like/As

DIRECTIONS: On a separate piece of paper, write out the following sentences correctly. If the sentence contains no errors, simply write a *C*.

1. Comma splices are where two complete sentences are joined by a comma.
2. My excuse for being lazy is because I don't like hiking.
3. A simile is when comparisons are made using *like* or *as*.
4. The reason I am not going to study hall is because I am on the honor roll.
5. Jeff thinks that Domino's pizza is better than Pizza Hut.
6. After Harry had played squash for two hours, his appetite is as huge as a bear.
7. When she is angry, Felicity's scowl is as mean as a bull.
8. Elise's trapping skills far exceed Ester.
9. Making the soccer team is one of the nicest things that has happened to me this year.
10. Because they pass often, Sarah and Eve are two of the most generous players on our team.
11. However, even those two girls could not help us, for we played one of our worst games last Wednesday.
12. Our opponents scored five of the easiest goals I've ever seen.
13. It was one of the most embarrassing moments of my life as goalkeeper.
14. Boston is busier than any city in New England.

15. Which book did you like best, *Moby Dick* or *The Scarlet Letter?*
16. Jane is stronger than any girl in her dorm.
17. Jerome is the most capable of the two writers.
18. After World War II, the U.S. was stronger than any country in the world.
19. When he speaks before the student body, Gerrard is so convincing.
20. This beach has so many rocks on it.
21. There is so much sugar in this coffee.
22. Jay has chosen such an interesting essay topic.
23. When I worked in the diner this summer, the kitchen was always so hot.
24. On every quiz, Andy gets a better grade than me.
25. Although I am older than her, Terry gets to stay out later.
26. If he gets to the den before me, Bo will certainly take the best seat for watching television.
27. This chess match will determine whether the computer is smarter than me.
28. If she was taller, she would be able to spike the volleyball easily.
29. I could get my driver's license if I was a year older.
30. He acted as though he was not responsible for the food spilled on the table.
31. If I was going to Big Y, I would buy some soda and chips for the picnic.
32. I wish that I was in the fall play, since that musical is my favorite.
33. Polly hasn't hardly any free time this semester.
34. The librarian can't help but appreciate your keeping the newspapers in order.
35. There wasn't scarcely enough food for everyone at our table.
36. The trouble with Belmont is that he cannot give anyone no respect at all.

37. With these new glasses, I can't hardly see the blackboard.
38. He cooks spaghetti like the Italians do.
39. Miranda sings like she is the star, but she has only a minor role in the opera.
40. From those clouds that are gathering, I think it looks like it is going to rain.
41. Laughing loudly, Maria sounds like she has had a wonderful time riding the skateboard.
42. By the end of the classroom day, I feel like I have run a marathon.
43. If I was thinking of resigning my job as treasurer, I would certainly tell the class president.
44. Shannon is by far one of the fastest skaters on the first line.
45. You may not agree, but I think that your brother is so hilarious.
46. That truck's tires are as high as a tractor.
47. If you can't run faster than me, you should expect to be passed on the track.
48. I could not hardly believe that Chris was going to wear that blazer to class.
49. Because there is no state-wide speed limit, drivers may go faster in parts of Montana than anywhere in the United States.
50. Once again it looks like the Mets will end up in the cellar.
51. I realized when I went to Crater Lake that nature can be so beautiful.
52. Some people can't help but be messy when they eat a bowl of soup.
53. I would not go to the mall if I was expecting to be bored.
54. In all respects, my father is a more experienced carpenter than me.
55. Grandma is one of my most generous relatives.

WORDS OFTEN MISSPELLED

acquire
among
argument
basically
beginning
breathe
business
category
character
choose
commitment
conscience
conscious
consistent
couplet
definitely
dilemma
disappearance
entrance
existence
experience
fault
forty
fourth
guerilla
grammar
hereditary
immediately
influential
initiative
innocent
intellectual

inference
knowledgeable
leisurely
led
liquor
marriage
medieval
noticeable
Negroes
occasion
occurrence
offered
passed
plague
playwright
possess
precede
prejudice
principal
proceed
psychological
pursue
quietly
receive
reference
referred
reminiscent
responsibility
reveal
rhyme
sacrilegious
safety

separate
sergeant
Shakespeare
significance
sincerely
solely
speak
specimen
subtle
succeed
succession
surprise
supersede
suppress
tolerance
traffic
tragedy
transcend
transparent
tried
twelfth
unnatural
vacuum
variation
vehicle
vengeance
vigilance
villain
welcome
whisper
yacht
yield

Others:

_____   _____   _____

_____   _____   _____

_____   _____   _____

_____   _____   _____

_____   _____   _____

_____   _____   _____

_____   _____   _____

_____   _____   _____

_____   _____   _____

_____   _____   _____

_____   _____   _____

_____   _____   _____

_____   _____   _____

_____   _____   _____

_____   _____   _____

_____   _____   _____

_____   _____   _____

_____   _____   _____

_____   _____   _____

THE WRITER'S CHECKLIST

THE WORDS

Write legibly. Avoid gross misspellings (SP):

a. Simple words (which, were, a lot, etc.);
b. Contractions (it's, who's, you're, etc.);
c. Words from the text you are writing about – the author, title, characters, places;
d. Common literary terms (tragedy, character, imagery, rhyme, rhythm).

THE SENTENCES

Avoid all forms of sentence errors (SE):

a. **Run-on** (RO) – two main clauses joined without punctuation or a coordinating conjunction (for, and, nor, but, or, yet – FANBOY);
b. **Comma splice** (CS) – two main clauses joined by a comma, without a coordinating conjunction;
c. **Fragment** (FRAG) – a word, phrase or dependent clause punctuated as a complete sentence.

Make subjects agree with verbs, and pronouns agree with their antecedents (AGR).

Give pronouns clear antecedents (PRO REF) and place modifiers close to the words they modify (MOD).

Avoid **awkward** (AWK) sentences by arranging your words in ways that are clear and not rough or ugly-sounding.

Fit your **sentences** together clearly and smoothly. (>)

Keep tense and person consistent. In all academic papers, use the present tense and avoid the first person singular.

THE WHOLE

Offer a useful **title**, remembering not to underline it or put quotation marks around it.

Introduce your **thesis** (central idea) logically.

Paragraph logically and usefully.

Transition – Have the first sentence in each internal paragraph introduce a new idea in a clear relationship with the previous paragraph's central point.

Back up your **arguments** with **examples** from the text.

Conclude your essay logically and smoothly.